D0547494

Dungeons and Drag Queens

Essays on Fire Island

through the eyes of its worst drag queen

GREG SCARNICI

Copyright © 2019 Greg Scarnici

www.gregscarnici.com

Edited by Bethany Bryan

All rights reserved, First Edition.

Cover photo by Magnus Hastings for #gayface

Cover design by Josh Wells and Gregory McMullen

ISBN: 9781793186669

DEDICATION

This book is dedicated to Angela Mercy, Anne Phetamine, Ariel Sinclair, Bambi, Beach DeBree, Bella, Bianca Del Rio, Boudoir LeFleur, Brenda Dharling, Bubbles D'Boob, Busted, Charity Charles, China, Cobra, Coco Love, Dallas Dubois, Demi Tasse, Dickie Addison, Donna Piranha, Ginger Snap, Gusty Winds, Hedda Lettuce, Holly Box-Springs, Holly Dae, Ivana Cocktail, Jacqueline Jonée, Lee Lee Heavenly, Levonia Jenkins, Lola Galore, Logan Hardcore, Margot, Kimmi Moore, Monét X Change, Nicki & Viva, Panzi, Philomena, Porsche, Robin Kradles, Rose Levine, Rosemary Potatoes, Sabel Scities, The Shapiro Sisters, Shequida, Sherry Vine, Sidonia, Stella D'Oro, Sweetie, Sybil Bruncheon, Tina Burner, Urban Sprawl, Whore D'Oeuvre, Yaneda Dunes, Zola and every drag queen who has ever graced the boardwalks of Fire Island.

CONTENTS

DISCLAIMER

Some of the names have been changed to protect the guilty.

FOREWARD: DON'T BE GAY

When I started the horrendous journey of trying to get this book published, I was met with resistance every step of the way. Agents I contacted told me a book about Fire Island was "too niche" aka "super gay." This even happened with the agents I knew who represented LGBTQ authors. A few of them told me publishers would only touch an essay collection by a gay guy if they had the visibility of Andy Cohen. Others told me that since only ten percent of the population was gay, and only like three percent of them knew about Fire Island, the book would be a hard sell because it was a "niche within a niche."

When I reached out to gay publishing houses, I was met with more resistance — but of a different kind. Apparently, shape-shifting romance novels (?) were big in the gay community, but since the only shape-shifters in my book wear fishnet stockings, they all passed. If only I had known that a book about a schoolteacher who morphs into a wolf and has an affair with a marine were so sought-after *before* I started writing this.

I thought of scrapping the book and starting a new one with a broader appeal, but then I got to thinking: Why the fuck would I waste my time writing about a shape-shifting porn star werewolf? Or write something with the sole intention of appealing to a mainstream audience? Commercial success has never been the driving force for my creativity. Expressing who I am and making work that comes from a gay perspective are. Besides, it's 2019. I shouldn't have to deny who I am by writing about something straight people or a select group of gay nerds are interested in. Instead, I'll write about something a select group of gay *sluts* are interested in!

Not to play "woe is me," but one thing that sucks about being a gay artist is that if you create work that comes from an LGBTQ sensibility, the industry will automatically assume your audience will be small. And there's some truth to this. I mean, if I were straight and wrote an essay collection about my disastrous Tindr dates, my audience would be a lot bigger. But since I write about things that come from my own, very gay experience and perspective, I get labeled "niche" right out the gate.

For this reason, I decided to self-publish this book, because something tells me there is an audience for a book about a gay guy who dresses in drag and hooks up on Fire Island while someone ODs on his roof deck. And if there isn't, IDGAF. This book cost me nothing to publish. And I'm going to get seventy percent of the royalties instead of like, thirty. So take *that*, shape-shifting schoolteacher werewolf author guy! Plus, since I can advertise to my "niche" audience on Instagram for like twenty bucks, I can be sure this book will reach the seventeen people who might be interested in reading it.

Hopefully you are one of them. If not, *stop reading this already. Jeez.*

- Greg Scarnici – January 2019

INTRODUCTION:
THE ISLAND OF MISFIT BOYS

Often described as a magical, heavenly paradise, Fire Island has been a major part of my life for over twenty-five years. Now, when I say "Fire Island," I'm of course talking about Cherry Grove and Fire Island Pines, the two gay resort towns on this slender barrier island off the southern coast of Long Island, cuz you know I don't visit those straight towns riddled with *Jersey Shore* rejects, and — ugh — children.

Both The Grove and The Pines have long been adored for their natural beauty, and for being lands of decadence and debauchery. Come here and you can create any experience you want — from long walks on the beach as deer prance along the sand, to a three-day, meth-fueled orgy where you wind up being helicoptered off the island to the nearest hospital. Choose your own adventure!

Although many think the heyday of Fire Island was the 1970s, when mustachioed men were running around in speedos having orgies everywhere, its history stretches all the way back to 1880, when Arthur and Elizabeth Perkinson opened the first hotel after they bought the land that is now Cherry Grove and Fire Island Pines for twenty-five cents an acre. Slowly, but surely Cherry Grove started forming into a community after the hotel went up. Soon after that, the boardwalks that make up the town's walkways were added, along with a post office. Then, just when Cherry

Grove was about to take off, the Great Hurricane of 1938 ravaged the town, turning a lot of people off from settling there.

A few years later, The Grove became a destination for gay artists and other social outcasts from New York City when they discovered it was a safe haven for the LGBTQ community. Word soon got around in theater and arts circles that Cherry Grove was a beautiful and fun-packed place to escape the city on weekends, a tradition that continues to this day.

When The Grove reached its maximum capacity in the 1950s and 1960s, a lot of gay men started calling Fire Island Pines their home when new construction brought in a lot more housing. Since it's three times the size of The Grove and was founded during the era of midcentury modern design, the houses are much larger and more architecturally superior to the simple bungalows of The Grove, although I'm sure you'll find a lot of people who prefer the run-down, shabby chic quaintness of Cherry Grove.

For this reason, The Pines has always attracted a more professional, and, dare I say, wealthier set of gay men, who pay more for their impeccable summer homes, which are peppered with equally impeccable men. In The Grove, you're more apt to find six broke drag queens sharing a room in a sublevel shack filled with black mold and glitter; whereas a summer share in The Pines will probably be filled with twelve muscle studs arguing over whose turn it is to empty the dishwasher. A dinner party in The Pines might consist of a fine rosé served with heirloom tomatoes over a bed of arugula and a main course of pork loin with grilled asparagus (no carbs **EVER**!), while in The Grove, you'll probably get invited to a dinner party where the only things served are potato chips, a bottle of Georgi vodka and some sassy reads. In The Pines, they pump Truvada into the tap water and the entire beach is air-conditioned! In The Grove, you're lucky if you can bum a Walgreen's aspirin and the only air-conditioning comes in the form of an eighty-year-old drag queen snapping her fan at you at the legendary Ice Palace nightclub.

One similarity between the towns is that most people who come to Fire Island have to rent a house with friends or in some cases, strangers. In The Pines, you might find yourself sharing a house with twelve guys, half of whom you don't even know. A lot of these shares are only for half or a quarter of the season because it can get really expensive to rent a house all summer long. In The Grove, the homes are a lot cheaper, and most accommodate just four to six people.

For example, my common-law husband, Paul and I currently share a full-season rental with our friend Carl in Cherry Grove. It's nice to be able to stay as long as we like without having to pack everything up before the next group of gays sashay in. (By the way, I refer to Paul as my common-law husband because it makes us sound like we belong on *Maury*. Also, after twenty-five years, I feel stupid calling him my "boyfriend" and "partner" makes it sound like we run an accounting firm. Also, all these uppity queens who got married now that gay marriage is legal get all bent out of shape when I call him my husband. I mean, girl, chill. We've been together longer than you've been alive.)

A lot has been said about "The Pines vs. The Grove" and in the past few years, the two towns are starting to seem a lot more alike. New construction in The Grove has brought in some modern homes that actually *aren't* covered in vinyl siding, and The Pines has started embracing a more carefree vibe, hosting drag brunches and events usually found in The Grove. And nowadays, you are just as apt to find someone ODing from GHB at a tea dance in The Pines as you are at an underwear party in The Grove!

Whichever town you find yourself drawn to, the allure of Fire Island for a lot of people is the opportunity to vacation in a place where you can be yourself without the fear of being attacked. There's a freedom that exists in gay enclaves like Cherry Grove and The Pines, and sadly, towns like these were needed for many decades before the LGBTQ community started gaining wider acceptance in society.

During a trip to either town, you're just about guaranteed to stumble across a drag queen drunkenly clomping down the boardwalk, as you decide whether to check out the busted beat dripping down her face or the amazing amber skyline calling to you from the bay. And any trip through the forest between Cherry Grove and The Pines (a cruising area known as the Meat Rack) will usually reveal a precious deer foraging in the woods or two bears 69ing in the sand. Toss in a gorgeous, ever-changing beach and jaw-dropping sunsets, and it's easy to see how Fire Island cast its spell over so many people over the years.

No rumination on Fire Island would be complete without mentioning its sexual energy. At any time, day or night, sex can be found — whether by cruising the boardwalks, meeting a handsome man at a tea dance, blowing a tick-ridden stranger in the Meat Rack, finding drunken trade at the late-night Dick Dock, having an orgy in the back room of the infamous Underwear Party, or by using what has become the go-to choice for hookups, apps like Grindr and SCRUFF.

A lesser-known fact about Fire Island is that a lot of men have converted second bedrooms and pool houses into sex dungeons and playrooms, and I have been lucky (and sometimes cursed) to have been inside some of them. Sex is always in the air — an energy that's heavily permeated the island since the 1970s.

I first started coming to The Grove when I was nineteen, mainly because it was a place I could be myself without fear of being taunted or attacked. Back in the '90s, you could get gay bashed just for walking down the street with a little too much swish, but on Fire Island, you were free to prance around like a runway model in a neon G-string lip-synching to Madonna without anyone so much as batting an eyelash. If you wanted to, you could also *kiss your boyfriend* without getting punched in the face.

As I started spending more time in The Grove, I discovered there was something else about the island that was pulling me in. Cherry Grove has always had a subversive undercurrent running through it, something you sense once you start getting to know the people who live, work and vacation there. This attitude dates all the way back to the 1940s, when The Arts Project of Cherry Grove started producing shows that parodied popular Broadway plays featuring men in drag.

During our first trips to the island, Paul and I started hanging out with various characters we saw whenever we visited. Like Peaches, a colorful old queen who covered himself in ropes of gold jewelry; Charity Charles, a drag queen who started performing on the island in the 1960s; Johnny Pool, a bartender who began slinging cocktails at the Ice Palace in 1964; China, a drag queen known for her shock of white hair and insanely dark tan; and Tommy Tush, who got his nickname from wearing speedos as a cocktail waiter. All these people came to the island because it was a place they could be themselves without putting on a façade. After a day at the beach, Paul and I would look for these eccentric personalities while having drinks at the Ice Palace, Sunsets, Tides and Cherry's on the Bay to share some laughs before heading home.

The wacky, carefree energy found in The Grove has vastly informed my outlook on life, as well as a lot of my work — whether it's my gender-fuck drag queen alter ego, Levonia Jenkins (hideously pictured on the cover), the videos and short films I have shot on the island, or this very book, which was written as I listened to the surf and tried not to check my SCRUFF notifications every eight seconds. For this reason, Cherry Grove has a special place in my heart. It taught me to embrace the subversive counterculture that's been circulating through the town since the 1930s and synthetically weave it into my work.

During the summer of 2010, I coproduced a short film called *Children of the Dune*, with my friend, Josh Rosenzweig. The satirical film, about a group of murderous, ragtag children who seek revenge on the vapid men who cast them aside once the trend of raising children has grown passé, was shot entirely on Fire Island.

At the end of the film, legendary (read = old) drag queen Sherry Vine makes an appearance to let the children know a magical home awaits them just a few feet from their camp in the Meat Rack. Her monologue completely sums up how I feel about Cherry Grove.

SHERRY VINE

"Children. Always disguising your pain through humor and violence! Well there's no reason to do that anymore. Because you are, and always will be, in a place where you are loved. Yes, my dear children of the dune, you are home! For just a few steps away lies a town called Cherry Grove, which is a land full of freaks, misfits . . . and alcoholics! A magical place, where time stopped in the year 1978. A place where transsexuals frolic on the beach with bearded lesbians, while men with handlebar mustaches run around in Jordache cut-off jean shorts, as Whitney Houston remixes play on a continuous loop!"

Although the monologue was intended to be comedic, any visitor to The Grove will tell you it could also serve as the town's Wikipedia entry. For some reason, The Grove never seems to change, and a Polaroid taken in 2019 could easily masquerade as one shot in 1979. The town has always been filled with misfits, outcasts, drag queens, cross-dressers, leather daddies, lesbians, transsexuals, musicians, DJs, actors, directors, writers, painters, photographers and artists — the people I am proud to call my non-gender-conforming brothers and sisters.

As someone who's felt like an outcast ever since I got a black eye trying to catch a baseball during my first day of Little League, I've always been drawn to people, places and things outside the mainstream. I feel most comfortable around other "freaks and misfits" who don't care about blending in. Cherry Grove is filled with these people. And that's why it's felt like home to me ever since I first visited in 1991.

On the following pages, I've assembled a collection of essays that shed light on some of the major events that take place during a typical summer on the island, and some of the memorable times I've had attending them. I've tried to touch on a lot of aspects of Fire Island life, like drag shows, tea dances, hookups, and how much of a pain in the ass it is to schlep everything on that fucking ferry. It's my hope that by the end of the book, you're inspired to visit Fire Island for the first or fiftieth time. For at any given moment, you just might find yourself stumbling into a dungeon . . . with a drag queen.

Sunset over the bay in Cherry Grove, as seen from the Tiki Bar when I was probably wearing a leotard.

THE LAND OF NO

You would think resort towns that only have three months a year to make money would welcome tourists with open arms — especially small communities on a thin barrier island people have to take a twenty-minute ferry ride to get to. But not Fire Island. For some reason, it seems the towns there do everything they can to *dissuade* day-trippers from visiting. Up until a few years ago, some towns didn't have public bathrooms and none rented beach chairs or umbrellas. After wondering why this might be, I discovered the island was inundated with lowlifes in the 1970s who came to drink, do drugs and have sex all over the place.

Most towns made changes to deter these dirtbags from visiting, and some even instituted laws to keep them at bay. In fact, Ocean Beach, a town located 3.7 miles away from Cherry Grove, became known as "The Land of No" because of all the rules the town implemented. "No Frisbees, kites, ball playing or radios. No picnicking. Must have shoes and a shirt on at all times." It's kind of ironic this town exists so close to Cherry Grove, where you can skip along the shore naked, high on mushrooms, while singing "Edelweiss" at the top of your lungs, day or night.

Before I called the kooky and carefree Cherry Grove home, I found myself in "The Land of No" when my friends and I rented a house there during the summer of 1991. Due to a recent hurricane, we were able to rent a place for a bargain, since a lot of the homes were damaged in the storm. And, thanks to said hurricane, the house in front of ours fell down, so ours was now ocean front-ish. Sure, all those absurd rules made our time there kind of a bore, and the destroyed house in front of ours was depressing AF, but that trip will always hold a special place in my heart because it introduced me to Fire Island.

My attraction to the beach actually goes back further than that. As an Italian-American from Queens, New York, the shore has always been a major part of my life. Some of my earliest memories are of trips to Jones Beach with my family when I was a kid. On stifling summer days, my mother would crank up the AC in our teal blue Malibu Classic, pack salami sandwiches and a cooler of iced tea, and we'd take the forty-minute trek from our home in Bellerose, Queens to Jones Beach. We'd spend our days lying in the sun, swimming in the ocean and listening to disco on WKTU. On the way back, I'd fall asleep as the air conditioner hit my sunburnt face and my saint of a mother battled traffic to get us home in time for dinner.

Looking back, I actually never got sunburnt. Since I'm Sicilian, I quickly transition from my natural olive state to browner-than-the-shit emoji in ten minutes — especially when I was a child and SPF was unheard of. In those days, we'd lather ourselves up with suntan *oil* and a bizarre concoction my sister made with iodine, Coca Cola and soy sauce, which turned us darker than Tan Mom by the Fourth of July.

During high school, I kept going to Jones Beach with friends until I got to college, when we found our way to Ocean Beach. Since we were still too young to get in the bars, we spent our week at the house drinking and getting high. Back then, I used to make everyone play ridiculous games whenever we partied. One of my favorites was "Ashy Ashy." The rules were simple: Someone would lean their head back, light a cigarette and pass it around the room until the ashes fell on someone's face and they had to take a shot. This was also the summer Madonna's *Truth or Dare* came out and I was obsessed with making everyone play it whenever I could.

Thanks to the wonders of tequila, Truth or Dare took a fun turn one night and most of us wound up naked. It all started when someone dared me to hang from the rafters swinging my dick in people's faces — a dare I gladly accepted. After I *somehow* lost my grip and fell on the coffee table, I found myself covered in chips, salsa and . . . *Funyuns*. Don't judge, honey. We were high.

Since it was my turn, I dared my friends Leslie, Maria and John to take a shower with me so I could get that mess off my body. They accepted, and before I knew it, we were lathering each other up in a four-by-four plastic shower shell as my guy friends marveled at my ability to get girls to do these things with me. They'd soon find out John and I were gayer than glitter, while girls seemed to figure it out the second the two of us started raving about Jennifer Holiday's performance at the 1982 Tony Awards.

After we dried off, I convinced the three of them to go skinny-dipping. As we stumbled onto the beach, I saw a giant sand pyramid I made that afternoon, illuminated by a full moon. As we swam in the ocean, I realized my friend Leslie had chickened out and was watching us from the shore. When I tried to convince her to come in, I saw a police cruiser driving down the beach towards us. Since we were in "The Land of No", where skinny-dipping was illegal along with just about everything else, we ran out of the water to try to get away from them. But it was too late.

Like an idiot, I thought we could hide from them in the sand ditch I dug to make the pyramid, so we all jumped in. While the four of us were absurdly crouching in the hole, we heard a car door open and close. A minute later, an officer walked over and shined a light down on us.

"What's going on down there?" he asked.

Not sure of what to say, we all stayed quiet, until Leslie, fueled by a little too much Jose Cuervo, leapt from the hole and screamed. "Go ahead! Is this what you want? To see us naked?! Well I don't care! Go ahead and look! I'm not ashamed of my body! This is me and I don't care!"

"Lady. I just saw some people stumbling out of the water and wanted to make sure you were okay," the officer said.

Leslie went silent. "Oh . . . I don't know what I was thinking!"

"You know, I could write you tickets for skinny dipping, but as long as you say you won't do this again, I won't," he said.

"Oh, without a doubt, Officer. We just arrived today and got a little out of control! I promise we'll be good!" Leslie said as he tried not to ogle her casually standing there naked. The rest of us started crawling out of the ditch, looking like breaded chicken cutlets from all the sand stuck to our bodies. We bid the officer goodnight and walked back to the house, now in desperate need of another shower.

Later that week, I was thrilled when Leslie suggested we go to Cherry Grove for dinner. Since I was a closet case who was dying to get there since the second we landed, I was on board. We took a water taxi as the sun started setting over the bay, and when I stepped onto the dock in The Grove, I was in awe. Men walked around in speedos, lesbian couples held hands while eating ice cream and a drag queen was sitting on a garbage can singing "Memories." It was like we stepped into some magical, gay theme park with a really fierce Oscar the Grouch. Right then and there, I knew I would be coming back as soon as I found the courage to come out.

After I finally did come out to everyone that winter, I took my first trip to Cherry Grove as a full-fledged homo the next summer and said goodbye to "The Land of No" forever. The fact that there were bathrooms you could use and a grocery store you could buy lunch at made it an ideal place for a quick visit. I'd spend my days lying on the beach with friends and hitting the bars before heading home on a 9:30 PM ferry.

The next year, I started spending weekends at The Ice Palace hotel, where I got to know some of the eccentric personalities on the island. Slurping down frozen margaritas with drag queens in the middle of the day made me realize there was no other place I'd rather spend my summers. Witty banter, impromptu drag performances and an overall sense of freedom made me fall in love with Cherry Grove.

A few years later, Paul and I rented our first house in The Grove with some friends. We'd spend our days on the beach, and nights grilling up dinners and decompressing from life in NYC. That's when I got to understand the allure of the island beyond partying with drag queens. Long, lazy days on the beach, awe-inspiring sunsets and candle-lit dinners on our deck showed me what island life could be like. We continued renting houses with friends until the summer of 2008, when I started living in Cherry Grove all season long. To this day, I still skinny-dip at night with whomever I can convince to join me. But sadly, I can no longer convince anyone to play Ashy Ashy.

THE NATIVES ARE RESTLESS

Although a lot of homeowners and renters start coming to Fire Island as early as March, the official launch of the season is Memorial Day weekend. Temperatures are usually in the low seventies and it's too cold to go swimming, but it's always a great time to reconnect with friends at cocktail parties, tea dances and dinner parties. That is, until Sunday, when the island gets inundated with hordes of low-end Long Islanders from across the Great South Bay, who wreak havoc all over Cherry Grove.

As soon as the 9:30 AM ferry lands, the town starts swarming with dirtbags from the mainland wearing Ed Hardy hats, Crocs and "Bro 4 Bro" shredder tees that expose their tasteful neck and lower-back tattoos. By 7:00 PM, they're wasted out of their minds, throwing up on the boardwalks, getting into fistfights, and, worst of all, badgering DJs into playing Justin Bieber. Thankfully, they stagger away on the midnight ferry and are not seen again until the weekend after Labor Day, when, for some bizarre reason, they return for the Miss Fire Island contest, which marks the unofficial end of the season.

Why these people only seem to visit in droves at the beginning and the end of the season is beyond me. Do they spend every weekend at monster truck shows? Are they too busy getting their faces tattooed? Does Costco give away extra Cheez Whiz samples on the weekends? I'll never know. Regardless, I'm always thrilled when that last ferry leaves at midnight, with what seems like every person who's ever gotten a paternity test on *The Jerry Springer* Show as we all scream, "Gurl, byeeeeeeee!"

DRAG ATTACK!

Parody, drag, subversion and humor have always been a part of Cherry Grove, and in my opinion, the quintessential spirit of the town is captured in an annual event called Drag Attack!, held on the first day of summer. This tongue-in-cheek "pageant" was created by Johnny Pool, a bartender who began slinging drinks on the island in 1964. At the tender age of 76, Johnny is *still* mixing drinks on the island and has since become one of the most well-known personalities in Cherry Grove.

Johnny held the first Drag Attack! in 1974, and continues to host the event to this day. Actually, it's hosted by his "sister," Cess Pool, because it's the one time a year he takes off his toupee to toss on a wig to get dressed in drag. Drag Attack! is a ridiculous send-up of typical drag pageants that crowns "The Worst Drag Queen In Cherry Grove." Glamorous drag is frowned upon, while bizarre, twisted drag is rewarded. While a monstrous costume will get you far, a clever name and one-liner during the question and answer round just might snatch you the crown.

Johnny told me he decided to hold the contest at 4:00 PM on a Tuesday, after the last ferry left so no one would see him in drag. Now, years later, he no longer cares that boats run until 10:00 PM, and that the event is packed with just about anyone who finds themselves on the island that day.

Me in a cheap Drag Attack! lewk with Johnny's alter ego, Cess Pool.

Although Drag Attack! has been going on since the 1970s, my friends, Bring It, Jose and I didn't discover it until 2007. Since then, we've entered the competition every year. Some of the characters we've shown up as include Tutu Much, an overweight ballerina in a tutu; Major Tourettes, a foul-mouthed drag queen in a majorette costume; She Mail, a postal "woman" during the Word Police Scandal of 2014; Crystal Meth Gayle, a long-haired mess of a drag queen who kept ranting and raving; Dick Pig McGee, a pig-nosed clown with a dress made of pictures clipped from gay porn magazines; Alicia Skeeze, a cornrowed diva who parodied Alicia Keys' hits; Tit Uncommon, a three-breasted Egyptian queen; HermAfroDite, a Greek goddess with a blonde afro and a giant dildo hanging out of her dress; Kim Carcrashian, a battered and bruised version of the famed reality star and BanAnna Wintour. What can I say? We like wordplay.

*Bring It as the tasteful Tit Uncommon, yours truly as She Mail
and Jose as Strawberry Short Bus at Drag Attack! in 2013.*

For years, the show was co-hosted by Charity Charles, a drag queen who started performing on the island in the 1960s. Recurring judges include China, a drag queen whose tan is as dark as her wig is white, and Tish, a bartender who likes to dress in high-society Boston drag, in honor of his hometown. You may be able to surmise that everyone I just mentioned is *old*. Johnny is 76. Tish, who still bartends on the island, is 66. Charity, who currently hosts drag shows in Fort Lauderdale, is 76; and China, who still parties until the early hours of the morning, is "somewhere between eighty and death."

I can still remember the night I walked China home at 4 AM because she couldn't make it down the ramp of the Ice Palace in her high heels — a feat I can barely manage at 4 *PM*. Or the time I went on a friend's boat at 2 AM for a nightcap and found China passed out on the floor. Or, on every Fourth of July, when she can be found at the Ice Palace, cocktail in hand, getting ready to board the ferry for the annual drag Invasion of the Pines at noon.

Needless to say, she is my spirit animal and I want to be her when I grow up. And if I don't magically morph into her, I'll settle for Johnny, Charity or Tish. Since they came of age in the 1960s, they're all open-minded, counterculture and cutting-edge, even to this day.

China judging Drag Attack! when she was a mere 141 years old.

It's no surprise my friends and I gravitated towards these characters the first time we entered Drag Attack! As a goof, I would give the judges "bribes" like envelopes with a dollar bill inside them, or long, flattering letters about how much I loved them. They all got our sense of humor and have honored us with first, second and third place practically every year we've competed. I'm still not sure if this has been a blessing or a curse, since I have to display the tacky gold blender, two-foot crumbling statue and solar pool cover sash that serve as the prizes in my living room until I'm able to return them the next year. That's the thing about Drag Attack! It's so campy that winners have to *return* the prizes the next year.

Me as Yvonne Simmons Winning Drag Attack! in 2010.
Yeah, I know the name wasn't a pun, but I carried around a ventriloquist puppetdressed in drag with a matching dress, so save it.

Although Paul doesn't dress in drag except for the Invasion, he loves it just as much as I do. The two of us started going to Fire Island in 1993 when we first began dating. In those days, we'd take day trips a few times every summer, and Paul loved watching drag shows, which were harder to catch because they weren't held every five seconds like they are today. Back then, you were more apt to see a drag queen partying in a bar than doing an hour-long show. It was always a delight to pop into the Ice Palace and find China twirling on the dance floor, cocktail in hand.

A few years later, Paul and I started renting houses with friends every August. That's when we started getting a lot more enmeshed in Cherry Grove culture and were able to call most of the drag queens like China and Charity our friends. Paul loves Fire Island just as much as I do — maybe even more — since he gets to work in his garden all summer long. Every weekend, he spends hours tending to his plants, hopped up on coffee, with our cat, Venus. He also loves having people over for dinner parties while using the tomatoes, jalapeños and basil he grows in the garden.

A few years after getting to know Tish, Johnny, and Charity, Paul and I decided to invite them over for dinner. We chose a Wednesday because it's the slowest day of the week and everyone was off from work. That day, we spent the afternoon on the beach, and headed back to our house at six to take showers and get ready for the dinner party, which was supposed to start an hour later.

When we got home, I took my bathing suit off on the deck and threw it on the railing to dry. As I slid the screen door open to head into the house, I heard Tish's inimitable voice coming up our walkway.

"Looks like there's a full moon tonight, honey!" he said as I tied a towel around my waist.

"Come in!" I told them. "Paul's at the store and I just have to shower real quick. Make yourselves at home!"

While I was showering, I started wondering why Johnny and Tish showed up so early. Did I make a mistake when I invited them? Were they just really old and hoping to get home by nine o'clock? When I finally got dressed and joined them for a drink a few minutes later, I found out why.

"Sorry we're early. We were smoking hash and drinking all day and I could have sworn that clock said 6:45!" Tish said as he took a sip of the martini Paul made him.

Lord. While I usually wouldn't think of having a drink until five, these men — who had 30 years on me — were smoking hash and drinking all day. On a Wednesday.

Charity joined us an hour later (aka on time.) By now, we were on our second rounds of drinks and the night was taking a fun turn. "Oh. I brought dessert. But I think we should eat it *before* dinner," Johnny told us. "They're pot brownies and that lasagna is gonna taste so much better after we eat them!"

Once again, I was deflated. These elders of Cherry Grove were making me feel like such a nerd. I stopped smoking weed in my twenties, and the last time I had a pot brownie was in Amsterdam in 1995, when I turned more paranoid than a conspiracy theorist on Facebook. Like an idiot, I forgot edibles take time to get into your system and ate two of them before we even sat down for dinner.

"Someone's in for a fun night!" Tish said as we made our way to the dining room table.

Over the course of the night, we learned a lot about our friends as we swilled bottle after bottle of wine. Somewhere around the time the lasagna came out, I started feeling buzzy and tingly and realized I was totally high. After we ate, we headed to the living room and listened as Johnny and Charity told us stories from their wild days. Although Charity always performed to old show tunes, she told us she did porn in the 1970s in Los Angeles. Johnny told us about his carefree days in San Francisco, and about the drug-fueled, cross-country trips the two of them took. By this point, I was literally so high my eyes couldn't focus, but Johnny, Tish and Charity kept reaching for the wine as they told us stories of Fire Island past. Paul ate up all their tales as he let out one of his infectious cackles every few minutes, which never fail to make me laugh.

Finally, our last bottle of Chianti dribbled its last drop and it was time to bid our friends goodnight. I looked at my watch and saw it was 1 AM. By now, I was completely gone, and realized that in addition to having thirty years on me, these people also had about five more hours of partying than I did and were doing fine. Sort of.

They stumbled out of our apartment and within seconds, I crawled into bed. I closed my eyes and passed out for ten hours. When I groggily woke the next day, feeling like the walking dead, I came to the sad realization we were out of eggs and that I'd have to go to the grocery store to make breakfast.

While I was walking into town, I ran into a bright and chipper Johnny, who was on his way to work.

"Fun party!" he said, seemingly in a much better state than I was.

"Oh, my God. You seem so awake right now. How do you do it?" I asked him.

"I'll tell you a secret," he said. "Every morning I start my day off with a little Kahlua in my coffee and it makes the day *a lot* better."

I laughed and continued on my way to the grocery store. Then I got to thinking. A little hair of the dog was probably just what the doctor ordered, so I went back to the bar and had Johnny make me one of his world-famous Bloody Marys. Turns out he was onto something. My hangover was gone in three sips.

LAWNGUYLIND

In order to get to The Grove or The Pines, you have to board a ferry in Sayville, Long Island and take a twenty-minute ride across the Great South Bay. Cars aren't allowed, so the only way to get there is to take the ferry and then walk around the boardwalks to get around town. The fact that there aren't any cars makes Fire Island peaceful and so far-removed from life back in NYC.

There aren't a lot of stores in either town, so you have to schlep just about everything you need for your trip on that ferry — unless you want to pay a huge markup at either of the grocery stores. One of my favorite things about taking that ferry is being able to eavesdrop on the conversations people have while riding it. Since The Grove attracts a diverse group of visitors, there's always a plethora of interesting people you might have the pleasure of overhearing. Unlike the ferry to The Pines, where you'll probably be riding with seventy-five middle class, cisgender gay dudes who are all talking about CrossFit and rosé, when you visit The Grove, you get thrown onto a boat with people of all races, shapes, genders and social classes discussing *all sorts* of things.

To me, the most fascinating people who ride the ferry are the ones who live on Long Island. Suffolk County is filled with lots of colorful characters: lesbians with purple porcupine haircuts, gay men with purple porcupine haircuts — and their hairstyles are almost as extreme as their accents. Listening to them talk is always wildly entertaining.

I've heard some of the most over-the-top accents on that ferry. Think Joe Pesci in *Goodfellas*, Joan Cusack in *Working Girl* or, more precisely, a gangster in a 1930s Bugs Bunny cartoon. What makes these accents even more absurd is that they're coupled with the gender-nonspecific vocal intonations of various gay, lesbian and trans men and women, making it hard for me to tell if that person going off on their housemate is a lesbian from Huntington, a gay guy from Hauppauge or a trans woman from Babylon.

In my years of cruising back and forth, I've heard the most unbelievable conversations I wouldn't hear anywhere else in the world in inflections you can't even begin to imagine. I've listened to a bisexual couple from Long Beach bargaining over what type of behavior would be acceptable once they got to the island ("If I see a gorl and I'm into huh, I'm gonna tawk to huh!"). I overheard two elderly lesbians from Mineola arguing over who would get to ride the jazzy once they got off the ferry ("My sciatica's been actin' up ever since I bawt all that Comet at tha Dollah Staw!"). And who could forget the time that gay guy kept talking about how much he loved his "boyfriend's motha's brothah's lovah's brothah" — a relation I'm still trying to wrap my head around fifteen years later.

While eavesdropping on these conversations is one of my favorite pastimes, listening to conversations people are *intentionally* trying to make me hear is one of my least favorite things in the world. Too many people use the ferry as a vehicle to put on scenes for the captive audience around them. They'll screech at the top of their lungs, carrying on as if they're on stage while taking "secret" glances to see if anyone is listening. Making it worse, these thirst-mongers are always surrounded by hangers-on who laugh way too loudly at everything they say, making sure everyone knows what an *amazing time* they're having. It's exhausting.

Even though there are tons of attention-starved LGBTQ Long Islanders — or Lawyn-guy-linders as I like to call them — on that ferry, there's one outrageously loud woman who makes them all pale in comparison. The first time I found myself on the same boat as her, I wanted to jump in the bay ten minutes into the "conversation" she was screaming at her "friend." To give you an idea of just how loud she is, I was listening to music on my iPhone ten rows behind her, and I *still* heard every word out of her mouth. I was in awe as I listened to her twenty-minute, stream of conscious rant that involved fishing, lawn chairs, renting her house, knee replacement surgery and *dawgs*.

"Yah nevah gonna believe this one!" she began. "I had ta bring out new lawn chayus to tha eyelind cuz them rattan ones rotted over tha wintah and tha guys at tha ferry charged me an arm ind a leg to delivah 'em! I'm tellin' ya, thank Gawd I got them on sale at Cawstco cuz I woulda told them to shove them damn chayus right up their asses! Ugh! This eyelind cawsts so much, but I keep coming back cuz I rent my place out and I gotta turn tha house ovah every Friday. I'm not payin' for some maid service cuz that's a ton of crap! You know how hard that is for me with this knee replacement? I can hardly wahk around, and now I gotta schlep fuckin' lawn chayus to this shit-hole and clean tha house! And when I get there, I gotta listen to my neighbor's dawgs bawkin' awl day lawng! Yappy little gay dawgs! I hate them! Right now, I wish I was fishin' in Bayshaw with my friend Lucy. Alls I gotta do is ride my cawr up to huh house on the bay, sit there and cast my loin awl day lawng with a Bud Light. But now I gotta ride this hunka metal to Tha Grove! Ugh!!" she screamed at the dazed man, who just stared at her blankly, unable to get a word in edgewise.

For the next fifteen minutes, we all had to listen as she bitched in an accent that made Fran Drescher's character on *The Nanny* seem refined.

"Don't get me stawted on tha bawrs! What a rip-awf!"

"Now I gawta get this othah knee replaced! It's gonna cawst me a fortune!"

"Alls we need is anothah hurricane and this whole damn eyelind is gonna be a scrap heap in tha ocean!"

By the time the boat docked, every passenger had descended to the lower level to get away from her. Not that it mattered. As we waited to disembark, we could *still* hear her screaming from up top.

"Lawd, now I gawta pay that rip-awf awtist twenty bucks to get these lawn chayus to my house from da boat. I'm telling you! Everyone's gawta angle out hee-yah."

Ironically, her name is Grace. She has a dry, brittle perm, the body of Tweedledee and looks like she buys all her clothes at Sam's Club. Since some of you who have been to the island might be thinking I just described eighty percent of Cherry Grove, let me be more descriptive. She's that loudmouth who waddles all over town as she scream-talks at people on her *eye*phone all the time.

Thankfully, I only run into Grace a few times a season, since I know her schedule and do everything I can to avoid riding that 11:30 AM boat on Fridays, when she comes to turn her house over. Besides being able to avoid her rants, it also means I'll be able to eavesdrop on *other* people's conversations, and hopefully find out what's been going on with that guy's "motha's brothah's lovah's brothah."

SERVING SUFFOLK CUNTY REALNESS

I always thought that if I were to come up with a drag queen alter ego, her name would incorporate some kind of wordplay. Something like what my friends Hedda Lettuce, Miss Understood, Gusty Winds or Lauren Ordair came up with. In my mind, I always thought my drag name would be something absurd and playful like Hagatha Christie, Pompadora the Explorer, Post Apocalipstick, Madame Mucil, Linda Hand, HermAfroDite, Angela Transberry, Natalie Wouldn't, or Helena Bottom Carter. As you can tell, I've given this some thought. But, alas, the drag name that got assigned to me was . . . Levonia Jenkins?

"Oh my God, Greg, can we talk about all the Suffolk County lesbians on that ferry?" was the first thing my friend Johnny said when I picked him up at the dock one afternoon. "I can't believe their accents and hairstyles! I've never seen anything like it! They all have the same spiky mullet and talk with the thickest accents!"

Turns out, I was not the only person aware of this.

Leave it to Johnny to notice the same people on the ferry as me. It should have come as no surprise. Johnny and I have shared a similar sensibility ever since we were closet cases at Saint Francis Prep high school in the late '80s. We were both into new wave and hung out with the "alternative" crowd. Johnny was a year older than I was, but all the freaks hung out together regardless of what class they were in. Johnny never failed to crack me up when we hung out, and over time, his sense of humor has gotten even better from writing about pop culture at TMZ, Dish Nation and a bunch of other entertainment sites and outlets.

Back in high school, I used to make low-budget movies by shooting them on a used camcorder and editing the footage together with two VCRs. Johnny starred in one of my favorites where he played a sex addict with a giant package who terrorized teenage girls in South Hampton. I think his tagline went something like, "You ever been with a Latin lovah?" as he wagged the eggplant we stuffed in his sweat pants back and forth. Johnny and I had a history of coming up with ridiculous projects whenever we hung out, which is why I was excited to get him on Fire Island, where creative projects come about magically all the time.

Shockingly, it was Johnny's first trip to the island, and even though he had grown up in Queens, years of living in Los Angeles had isolated him from this very specific facet of the LGBTQ community. (Side note: I still think the Q in LGBTQ is ridiculous. I mean, if you're questioning your sexuality, just get back to me when you figure it out. And if you're using the Q to say you're queer, isn't that covered in the G or L?!?)

Thankfully, Johnny got to meet a lot of the lesbians he saw on the ferry the next night, when I brought him to Cherry's for a sunset disco party. I introduced him to some of the ladies I knew, and he had a great time getting to know them and realizing they were more than just women with porcupine haircuts. Lesbians. They're just like us!

I'm sure this works in reverse, too. Something tells me every lesbian probably looks at me and my friends and thinks, "They all have beards and buzz cuts and wear the same H&M bathing suit. And their Queens accents are over-the-top!" And they'd be right. While in The Pines you're only be judged by upper-middle class gay men, in The Grove, gay men, lesbians, bisexuals and trans people of all social strata judge you. It's that melting pot aspect that makes The Grove so special to me. Instead of interacting with a bunch of guys you probably see at the gym back in NYC, you get to meet people you might not meet anywhere else on earth. And have them silently judge you for wearing an H&M bathing suit as you share Fireball shots.

After we danced at Cherry's, Paul grilled up dinner on our deck and Johnny got to finally meet our housemate, Carl. The two of them hit it off instantly. A native of Massapequa, Carl has the most memorable Long Island accent and Johnny ate it up. Carl also has a high-pitched voice, and every single person I've ever introduced him to instantly falls in love with him and the way he *tawks* because he's such a lovable guy.

After dinner, the four of us watched Jennie Livingston's documentary *Paris Is Burning* for the eightieth time before we headed to the Underwear Party at the Ice Palace. Besides loving the ballroom scenes, we knew the movie would fuel us with one-liners we'd be able to toss out to strangers all night long.

The Underwear Party was created by a nightlife promoter named Daniel Nardicio in The Grove sixteen years ago. It slowly started growing bigger, with drag hostesses like Bianca Del Rio and fun late-night performances from downtown cabaret singers like Bridget Everett and a then-unknown Lady Gaga. Since then, the party has gotten huge, and every Friday night hundreds of men from The Pines take a water taxi to party in their Andrew Christian underwear.

The night we went there, Johnny and I used classic *Paris is Burning* lines as we screamed, "Tens! Tens! Tens! Tens! Tens across the board!" at a guy wearing a Nasty Pig jockstrap, and "Serving Suffolk County Realness" at one of the bartenders in a Day-Glo G-string. Somehow, *Paris Is Burning* and Johnny's newfound fascination with Suffolk County lesbians got thrown into a blender with that year's breakout hit *The Real Housewives of Atlanta* to conjure up the persona of Levonia Jenkins.

Johnny and I were obsessed with Dwight Eubanks, Kim Zolciak, NeNe Leakes, Sheree Whitfield and their catfights, wig snatches, and "Alter-Ego Photo Shoots." All weekend, we called ourselves "The Real Housewives of Fire Island" while pretending to throw wine in each other's faces and ripping each other's wigs off in between stints of referencing Suffolk County lesbians and quoting *Paris is Burning*.

Johnny in "Real Housewives" mode before I snatched off his wig.

We capped off our weekend by having brunch on our deck before Johnny headed back to LA. As we drank mimosas with Paul and Carl, we riffed on all the jokes we came up with that weekend. At one point, I snuck away from the table for one of my surprise drag "transformations." I crept into the bedroom, dug into my drag bag and found a gold lamé dress and a ratty wig I used for a Madonna parody I shot for YouTube a few years back.

Since the wig had been crushed under a bunch of polyester outfits from years of doing Drag Attack!, it looked like some sort of dead animal. I threw it on with a pair of sunglasses and the gold lamé dress, and sashayed onto the deck in clunky black-and-white shoes. Johnny was thrilled.

"Oh my God! It's like *Paris Is Burning* meets Long Island Suffolk County Lesbian Porcupine Haircut Realness!" he said as I started an impromptu dance to the Mary Jane Girls' "Candy Man" on the deck.

"Yes, queen! Work! And serve! And slam your weave into those tomato plants," he improvised as I drunkenly pranced around the deck.

"I *love* it!" shouted Carl as he guffawed.

"You are a *mess!*" Paul added.

"Wait! We should shoot a *Paris Is Burning* parody with this character!" Johnny announced.

Never one to shy away from the camera, I was down. Since this was years before everyone had a video camera on their cell phone, I reached for the Flip Video camera I brought to the island for just this kind of impromptu shoot.

Before I knew it, we were on the roof and Johnny was shooting the video as he screamed, "Live . . . from the roof of The Cherry Grove! Levonia Jenkins . . . serving it up . . . Fire Island Style!" as I "worked and served" to his *Paris Is Burning*-style chant.

After we were done, I asked Johnny where the name Levonia Jenkins came from as I ripped that sweaty mess of a wig off my head.

"I don't know. It just came to me!" He laughed. "It sounds like she could be from Babylon or Bensonhurst. Miss Levonia! Werking and serving it up at Auntie Anne's Pretzels at Roosevelt Field mall!"

I hooked the Flip Video camera up to my computer to post the video on YouTube. A few hours later, Perez Hilton saw the video and tweeted it out. Overnight, our raw, off-the-cuff video got 20,000 views.

Levonia Jenkins took off, mainly because she was a mess, could not vogue to save her life, and was accompanied by Johnny's hilarious pop culture commentary. We continued to shoot "Vogue Revolution" videos whenever we saw one another, and before I knew it, my drag persona was . . . Levonia Jenkins?

If I had my say, I would have liked to come up with a drag character and not have her created for me during a drunken afternoon. But looking back, I'm glad Levonia came into my life. People seem to love her ridiculous persona — loosely described as a woman you'd meet on the G train who's an R&B singer from the '80s who releases '90s-inspired house tracks?

In fact, when I die, one of my greatest accomplishments will be the fact that if you search the name of Levonia's first song, "So Cunt," her music video is the first hit that comes up on Google. Just to show you how insane the internet can be, when I released the video — which was a takeoff on a term gay men use to describe a drag queen who looks convincing as a woman — feminist blogs wrote it up, saying I was "reappropriating" an offensive term to make it celebratory. Considering the track was sung by a hideous drag queen with a beard "vogueing" on the F train, I'll take it.

Levonia Version 1.0 in 2009 wearing her gold lamé dress, ratty wig and a dildo? I know, you probably missed it because you're fixating on that hideous, rusty deck chair behind her.

BITCH, PLEASE
BY LEVONIA JENKINS

Gurl. You can keep trying to make these fools think you created me, but the reality of the shituation is that *I* created *you*. I mean, *really*. Levonz was at the clubs, dancing at the Paradise Garage and the Loft while you were still nomping on your momma's titties! All through the '80s, Levonz was carrying on in the clubs, learning her signacunture vogue moves from all the queens at the ball and getting style advice from Vanity 6 and Sheila E! Then, through the '90s, Levonz was in Brooklyn, taking a break from nightlife to nurse Auntie Janie, who was riddled with bunions, the poor thing. But that entire decade, Levonz was plotting her return to New York nightlife, and now, here I am! Back from the dead like one of those zombies the millenniums are into, werking and serving 4 tha chillrin!

So before you run around telling urrybody you *created* Levonz, you need to realize Levonia Jenkins is, was, and always will be *hurr*. I am the spirit of NYC, a combination of Mary J. Blige, Evelyn "Champagne" King, Willi Ninja, Pepper LaBeija, Dorothy Zbornak, Mayor Ed Koch, Alisha of "All Night Passion" fame, and Dee from *What's Happening!!!!* You can feel me when you ride the G trains, you can smell me when you eat a hot dog at Grey's Papaya and you can visit me at the deli counter at C-Town Supermarkets on the Lower East Side. So back up before I take this razor outta my mouth and cut you! Because I don't need no queen from Queens telling the whirl she created me on Tired Island cuz I am my own creation!

P.S.: Please do not retaliate by alerting Facebooks that I am a drag queen, because then my account will get deleted and I'll disappear like that witch at the end of *The Wizard of Oz* when they peed on her.

Levonia Version 20.0 at the Ice Palace during the Invasion in 2016.
Yes, I'm the one who put that fake bill in my bikini because no one ever tips me.

HURRICANE BRING IT

Years before the creation of Levonia and our discovery of Drag Attack!, my friends and I liked to dress in genderfuck drag whenever we were on Fire Island. I'm talking mustaches, beards, polyester dresses, and synthetic wigs. I recently found out the type of drag we liked to wear actually got its start in the Grove in the 1940s. Back then, drag was done with only a camp sensibility. The men wore dresses and wigs with full beards and had no interest in being "fishier than shrimp scampi," as the kids don't say. In the 1950s and 1960s, drag started to evolve, and a lot of men were turned off by the more polished drag queens who started showing up. I personally like all styles of drag, but am drawn to anything comedic or subversive, which is why I like genderfuck drag the most. There's just something about a hairy man in a sequined gown I find both amusing and thought-provoking.

That's why, whenever we were on the island, my friend Bring It and I would throw on large, ratted wigs and long T-shirts of a woman's nude body and do numbers for our friends in the living room. A restaurateur by trade, I believe Bring It missed his calling and should have been the next Rip Taylor. He is, by far, one of the funniest people I've ever met. He has long, curvaceous sideburns like Chris Kattan's Mango character from *Saturday Night Live* and always wears a backwards Kangol. His motto in life is: "Work hard and play hard." And he does: sometimes working twelve-to-fourteen hour days for weeks in a row. But when the time comes to party, he *parties*. His favorite drug of choice is the popular cat tranquilizer Special K, which instead of sedating him, makes him do drag shows set to '80s acts like Starpoint and Lisa Lisa and Cult Jam with Full Force. Even though I stopped doing drugs years ago, I love hanging out with him because being around him makes you *feel* like you're on drugs.

I first met Bring It when he was an ecstasy dealer at Body N Soul, a downtown party held in NYC in the '90s. In truth, Bring It wasn't really a drug dealer. He just knew where to get ecstasy and liked hooking up his friends. The first time the two of us met, he was seated on a couch in the Body N Soul lounge holding court with ten people hanging on his every word. I joined his crew and quickly realized what his attraction was. Bring It has the ability to make everyone laugh uncontrollably. That Sunday night was no exception and we became fast friends.

Paul and Bring It, wearing terrible living room drag in 2006.
I'm assuming Paul's crotch is wet because he was making dinner
and leaned against the sink, but who knows. Maybe he peed himself.

Bring It and I never went into town in Cherry Grove in our sloppy drag because it was just something we did to make each other laugh. Besides, whenever Bring It dresses in drag, he turns into a monster. He becomes like one of those Gremlins who get fed after midnight and it wasn't fair to sic him on unsuspecting people like that. If there was any doubt to this theory, we put it to the test one Sunday afternoon, when we decided to go out dressed in low-rent drag.

While Bring It and I were doing performances in our living room to Malcolm McLaren's "Madame Butterfly" and the Eurythmics' "Love Is A Stranger," Paul came back from the grocery store with a flyer in his hand.

"Hey, guys, looks like that woman who sang 'Doctor's Orders' is performing at Sunsets tonight," he said.

"I love that song!" Bring It said. "We should go in drag!" he announced as he started mixing up a pitcher of frozen margaritas. "Doctor's orders say there's only one cure for me . . . " he sang-warbled in the kitchen.

While he was blending the drinks, I looked for some disco-inspired outfits. I found a blonde feathered wig and a silver chain-metal halter top for myself, and a voluminous black wig and blue sequined jacket for Bring It. After we changed and put our wigs on, I threw some white powder on our noses so it looked like we were on a coke binge. Based on how Bring It was acting, that wasn't much of a stretch.

"Hi, honey, I went to see the doctor today!" he sang as he danced around the house, scream-singing.

The day of the tragic event. Note Bring It's signature sideburns.

The three of us headed to the bar so we could hear the actual biological woman who sang "Doctor's Orders" perform it, instead of Bring It, who was out-of-control wasted by this point. He made it to the bar and started torturing strangers by getting in their faces and lip-synching to all the disco classics they were playing before Carol Douglas came on. I joined him and the two of us started doing shows for the audience, who were all thinking, "Where the fuck did these two come from?"

When Carol Douglas finally came out, Bring It and I were front and center, singing right along. "DOCTOR'S ORDERS . . . SAY THERE'S ONLY ONE THING FOR ME," we shouted as Carol stared at us with a look of horror. Apparently, she was not pleased with our enthusiasm. When the song came to a close, Porsche, the drag queen hosting the show, came out to talk with Carol.

"Welcome to Fire Island!" Porsche said in her enthusiastic way. "Are you having a good time?"

"Oh, I always have fun on Fire Island. Even though the last time I was here was 1985!" Carol replied. "You know, this island never changes. Whether it's the sun going down over the bay . . . or that old drag over *there*!" she said as she pointed at us. Oh no! She was throwing us shade! Here we were, trying to support her by being so enthusiastic, and she was coming for us.

"That's right, honey! This old drag is gonna get me *aaaalllll* the dicks, too!" Bring It screamed as I turned red.

"Well, good luck with that!" Carol said as I tried to pull Bring It over to the bar for a shot. My ploy worked. Like a cat with a toy being dangled in front of its face, Bring It took the bait and joined me for a shot of tequila.

"Okay. I'm done with that tired hag anyway," he said far too loudly. Unfortunately, my plan backfired, and after the shot, Bring It picked up enough steam to turn into Hurricane Bring It — an obnoxious version of himself that doesn't slow down until it destroys everything in its path. Some people found Hurricane Bring It funny, but whenever he turned into this force of nature, Paul was mortified.

After Bring It walked up to a stranger, ripped his baseball cap off and threw it into the bay as he was putting on a show to Shannon's "Give Me Tonight," Paul was done.

"Okay, we're going home. We're having dinner and you need to sober up," he said as he pulled Bring It out of the bar by his wig. Knowing the jig was up, Bring It started acting like leaving was his idea.

"I was done with this shit hole *anyway*!" he screamed as he nearly fell off the boardwalk. "Now let's get home so I can put on a sensible outfit for whatever *slop* you're gonna serve me," he said as he laughed, kissed Paul on the cheek and won him back over.

The three of us went home and Bring It took a long, hot shower as Paul and I cooked dinner. When I went into his bedroom to let him know it was time to eat, he was passed out. Paul and I ate on the deck, and about an hour later Hurricane Bring It must have picked up steam over the Atlantic Ocean because he was now wearing some drag ensemble that made him look like the Bride of Chucky.

Bring It, thirty drinks in. And no, his eyes are not red from the flash.

"C'mon! Sherry Vine is performing at the Ice Palace, and I want to torture her," he said with a playful look in his eyes.

"Hell no," Paul told him. "Doctor's orders say there's only one thing for you and that's dinner!"

Bring It scowled, threw his wig on the floor and gave in. "Fine," he said as he looked down and realized there was food on the table. "Wait. Is that pasta? Gross. I'm watching my carbs," he said as reached into the bowl with a devilish grin on his face and started shoveling spaghetti into his mouth.

CUCKOO BANANAS

For some reason, Fire Island attracts some of the most insane people in the world. Many of them are day-trippers you'll see shopping for groceries in a neon pink mankini, but some of these people actually live here all summer long. A lot of them are performers, and sadly, their need for attention does not stop on the stage. They consider every boardwalk a performance venue. That corner by the real estate office? It's Radio City Music Hall! The ferry landing? Lincoln Center! And the grocery store? Well that, my dear, is the stage of the Lucille Lortel Thee-AY-ter!

I'll pass these lunatics on my way to get a sandwich, and see them having the most intense "conversation" with some captive person. I always exchange a sympathetic glance with these prisoners since I know what it's like to be seized by a maniac. I happen to have a lot of bipolar people in my life, and know what it's like to be followed around as they recount riveting, three-hour stories about their Metrocard not swiping.

Even worse are the people who are obviously *on* or *in need* of meds who get wasted out of their minds and turn into maniacs after their third drink. One second they'll be having a blast and then — WHAMMO — they're attacking people with bar stools.

I have yet to figure out why so many of these freaks are attracted to Fire Island. Maybe they like being big fish in a small pond? Maybe all gay people are theatrical? Or maybe it's just that people who are drawn to a place where you have to schlep absolutely everything you need on a fucking ferry are mentally imbalanced to begin with. At any rate, there are loads of people on Fire Island with overbearing personalities and cuckoo eyes, who make that day-tripper in the jockstrap and high heels singing show tunes as he eats chicken wings in the ocean seem downright normal.

MARCH MADNESS

It seems like every weekend, there's a fundraiser or huge event on Fire Island. It can truly be exhausting if you're the kind of person who likes to keep up appearances. But at the end of June, the town holds two events you can enjoy from the privacy of your own home as they prance right past your house. The first is the miniature Gay Pride parade, which runs for like fifteen minutes. That's a big change from the Pride parade in New York City, which takes place the following weekend and runs *nine hours* long.

Bars and restaurants decorate golf carts with balloons, and drag queens ride in the back of them, waving at people as they make their way through the downtown business district. Various characters from The Grove march between these makeshift "floats" and sometimes a person will hook up a speaker to play "I Am What I Am" and other Gay Pride ~~stereotypical garbage songs~~ classics.

One year, the theme of the parade was Gay Marriage. Couples marched with signs that displayed how long they had been together, and it was heartwarming to see couples announcing unions of fifteen, thirty and forty-five years. It's small, but touching, things like this that make living in a community like The Grove so wonderful.

The second parade-like event takes place the next weekend, when the Arts Project hosts a kooky fundraiser called the House Blessing, which also snakes through town. The bizarre procession continues the subversive nature of The Grove by mocking religion, while also reveling in it. Members of the Arts Project dress up in religious costumes and ride up and down every walk of The Grove on a fire truck while screaming, "House Blessing!" and ringing a loud bell. For a token contribution, they will bless your home by spraying it with "holy water."

Although the community is filled with lots of lapsed and practicing Catholics, no one gets offended that men dress up as nuns and women dress like bishops. It's really just another day in The Grove. And although I always seem to be hung over when they pass our house and clang that damn bell at 10 AM, I always bound out of bed to give them money so I can catch a glimpse of "Sister Phyllis" as she rides atop the fire truck to bless our homes.

THERE'S NO PLACE LIKE HOME

Most homeowners in the Grove have a playful name for their house, which they display at the entrance to their property. Many of these names reference gay culture or feature some kind of wordplay, like Morning Woods, Bottoms Up, Deer Abbey, Sumner Time and Big Dick's Halfway Inn. Other houses cull their names from fiction and folklore. In fact, a few steps away from where I currently live is a precious little property called Hansel and Gretel, which might be the most photographed residence in town.

I also like *giving* homes names, like Hipster Heights, a large complex on the beach that attracts lots of Brooklyn hipsters, and Meth Manor, a place where a bunch of meth heads are somehow able to scrape up enough money to share a place where they can smoke meth and work on "art projects" all summer long. What can I say? I like alliteration.

Hansel and Gretel in Cherry Grove.

HOMECOMING QUEEN

At the beginning of every season, the Arts Project of Cherry Grove ushers in the summer by electing a new Homecoming Queen. Any drag queen can enter, but since it's a popularity contest, queens who are either active in the community or who perform on the island are usually the ones who wind up snatching the crown. Then, throughout the season, the winner has to introduce *every single* event at the Community House, make appearances at various fundraisers, and bring an entire court with her to the Invasion on the Fourth of July.

Every summer, I think of entering the contest as Levonia Jenkins, but then she gets in my head and screams, "GURL are you out of your gay *mind*?!?!? That homecoming queen has to paint her face, slap on a human hurr wig and slip into an ensemble from Rainbow Shops for *every event* they have, and you can barely get into drags once a month!" Then I say, "Fuck it" and decide I'll only focus on trying to take home the crown during Drag Attack! and hopefully a sash during . . . the Invasion . . .

Logan Hardcore crowning Ginger Snap Homecoming Queen in 2017.
No, I do not know why this looks like a scene from Carrie.

THE INVASION

Cherry Grove has always sashayed to the beat of its own drum. In the 1930s and '40s, men would come to the island, dress in drag, and put on campy shows for their friends. Back then, cross-dressing was considered risqué, and men could only get away with doing it in secluded places like Cherry Grove without fear of being attacked or — even worse — arrested. Cut to seventy-five years later, when practically every gay guy has a drag alter ego and queens who perform on the island paint their faces on the Long Island Railroad without worrying about getting the shit beat out of them.

The town's long history of camp helps explain why the community celebrates the Fourth of July by gluing on lace-front wigs and donning ball gowns to board a ferry and invade The Pines. It's a Grove tradition created by Panzi, aka Thom Hansen, in 1976 that grows bigger every year.

In Thom's own words, "The Invasion began on July 4th, 1976 as a protest statement to John Whyte in the Pines, for refusing to allow Teri Warren in his establishment because she was in drag — he said it was a 'family restaurant.' Nine invaders boarded a small water taxi and exploded into the Pines Harbor at high tea. Today, the Invasion has swelled to over 300 cross-dressers and is an annual tradition in both communities, celebrating our diversity and joy of living: no politics, no organizations, just a day of plain fun." And what fun it is!

Although Thom says the event is not political, in the summer of 2017, he made his entrance dressed as a Mexican woman and burst through a wall of construction paper as he exited the ferry, and I showed up carrying a "severed Trump head," á la Kathy Griffin, that was beat to the gods with drag makeup. In my opinion, there are always some politics tossed into the mix of sequined gowns and billowing bouffants most queens don.

Regardless of whether you think the Invasion is political or not, the original act of showing up in drag and demanding service at an establishment is undoubtedly political. In my opinion, Terri and his friends are unsung heroes in the gay rights movement. By refusing to be discriminated against, they helped bring about a change in gay culture. In the 40 years since its inception, drag has gone from being an embarrassment to the gay community to something that is now celebrated with Emmy Awards on national television. For this reason, I will always celebrate the Invasion to honor its importance.

Levonia with Donna Trump, the Romper Roomies (aka Paul, Carl and Michael) and Johnny as The Handmaid's Tale at the 2017 Invasion. And yes, I was carrying that head around to try and distract from my tragic tuck.

Unfortunately, I didn't get to experience my first Invasion until 2010 because I always worked in New York City as a writer for the *Macy's Fourth of July Fireworks Spectacular*. After years of working on the show, NBC decided to bring in a new production company in 2010, and I found myself unemployed and on Fire Island that day. The night before the big holiday, I went out dancing with Carl, and let's just say we were not feeling our best when we woke up that morning.

While we were having breakfast, Carl started talking about the Invasion.

"I can't believe you've never been. It really is the best time ever! It's so much fun! We should do it today!"

I was not feeling it.

"What are you talking about? Queens work on their outfits for months and it starts in three hours!"

"Please. You have all that drag in that IKEA bag on the bottom of your closet! You can make us outfits!"

I wasn't so sure.

"All my drag is like $20 outfits from Rainbow Shop and cheap wigs I bought on 14th Street," I told him.

" . . . and? Who cares? It's not like we're trying to win prizes! And we get to drink for *free*!"

I was in.

I went to my closet, grabbed my IKEA bag of drag, and dumped it on the living room floor. I found an outfit for Carl in a snap: A red and black lingerie set with "Angel" imprinted on the top and a wig I used for a Britney Spears parody I did for YouTube. As I dug through the rest of my drag, I found the perfect outfit. The year before, I shot a parody of Madonna's *SEX* book on the island, and I still had one of her blond wigs, a pair of fake breasts, a merkin and a black fishnet dress. Perfect. I could go as Mandonna.

While tourists who had come to see the Invasion marveled at my "nude woman illusion," drag queens who spent months making their costumes and styling their wigs kept throwing me side-eye. I didn't care. Drag is about fun in my eyes, and if you only support one type of drag like pageant drag . . . gurl, bye.

Thankfully, there are lots of different styles of drag at the Invasion. The Imperial Court of New York always arrives in regal pageant looks. Someone always comes dressed as the Statue of Liberty, while others come in topical costumes like Caitlyn Jenner and Handmaid's Tale, like my friend Johnny. Since it's always hot and humid, many people (myself included) sometimes wear only bikinis, even though bathing suits are looked down upon as being *basic* in many queens' eyes. But since everyone in my family sweats so much we have to take salt pills, I ain't putting on no beaded gown when it's ninety degrees only to collapse from heat exhaustion!

At this point, people expect to see Levonia anyway, so I'm usually able to find an animal-print catsuit, slutty stripper outfit, or equally tasteless ensemble that will "fit her brand" while "giving the chillrin life." Thankfully, other drag artists like Brooklyn's Machine Dazzle do not overheat like at 1982 Toyota Tercel, and come dressed as pancakes and alligators in full-body costumes. Godspeed.

Carl and I had a blast the first time we did the Invasion, and have done it every year since. I have to give credit to Panzi, Philomena, Zola, China, and countless other drag queens who've done it practically every year since it was created — rain or shine. Thanks to these pioneers, the event has grown so big that, today, thousands of people come to the harbor in The Pines to cheer the drag queens on as they disembark the ferry.

Needless to say, the Invasion is insanely fun. The year after Carl and I first did it, we convinced Paul to dress up, and every year, we add more and more dragoons to our motley crew. Some of my favorite Invasion memories include:

• That time Paul fell off the boardwalk trying to walk in heels for the first time.

• That time Carl hooked up with someone while he was still in drag, then showed him out of the house when they were done with a fake eyelash stuck to his cheek.

• That time I barged into a stranger's party and did a performance around their pool which ended with me diving into the pool, wig and all.

• That time some idiot lit a firework off at the Sip N Twirl bar in The Pines, which set off all the fire alarms.

• That time we brought a megaphone to shout orders at people to get us drinks all day long.

• That time I was late to DJ in The Grove after the Invasion, so I just showed up in a speedo with my face still beat.

• That time I handed fake $100 bills to everyone at The Ice Palace, who tried to use the money to buy drinks.

• And, lastly, that time my friend Jack fell off the ferry in drag and we all took pictures of his wig floating across the bay as they fished him out of the water.

I'm pretty sure these memories go a long way in backing up Panzi's claim that the Invasion is "just plain fun!"

Showing up to DJ with my face still beat,
wearing a backwards baseball cap for that "Masc 4 Masc" lewk.

INVASION OF THE WIG SNATCHERS

A few years ago, I was asked to write an article for the now-defunct *Next* Magazine about my experience attending the Invasion, which I think does a pretty good job of describing what a typical day is like . . .

This year, I once again celebrated the 237th birthday of America by slapping on a sequin tube top, a synthetic wig and boarding a ferry with 200 drag queens to partake in the 37th annual Invasion on Fire Island. This year's event was greeted by gorgeous weather and, as always, hordes of locals and day-trippers gawking at the outrageous festivities.

Since I'm the official "drag queen" of my house, I was elected to do everyone's makeup. Oddly, my friends have not yet realized that my alter shego, Levonia Jenkins, is a hot mess who wears sunglasses most of the time because her makeup is so terrible. Regardless, at 10 AM, I start painting everyone's face, hoping they'll be happy with the Bozo The Clown-like appearance I am conjuring – and thanks to all the tequila shots they've been pounding; they are.

Before I know it, it's 12 o'clock. I glue on some lashes, zip up my boots and step outside. As sweat starts pouring down my face, I wonder why the hell I've decided to do this again. When we get to the Ice Palace, the reason hits me: the sight of hundreds of men dressed in fun, clever and ridiculous costumes is breathtaking. Highlights include local dragoons, Ariel Sinclair as a spot-on Paula Dean, Gusty Winds as a 60s-era flight attendant, and two men dressed in full hajibs, who my friend, dressed as Man-da Bynes, dubs The Real Housewives of Kabul.

I avoid getting on the ferry until the last possible second because there's nothing worse than sitting on a boat waiting for 200 drunk drag queens to board. I thankfully remember even though you'd think it would be nice to be in the sun during the ferry ride, it is horrifying. So downstairs we stay, where I run into drag diva, Peppermint and get inspired to do a pole dance.

Out of nowhere, the boat turns into the harbor and gets blasted with gale-force winds. My wig and 12" record beret go flying down the aisle – along with assorted crowns, fans and props that have also been whisked away. As I sit down to re-pin that damn record to my wig, I realize it's a blessing – the entire boat fills with a cool breeze and everyone breathes a sigh of relief.

Horns! Cheering! We're in The Pines! And I recall another reason I do this: There's something emotional about being cheered by thousands of people in the harbor as the boat arrives. The ferry docks and I instantly recall why I will never do this again: Waiting on that boat for 200 drag queens to exit is a nightmare. There's no air, sweat pours down my body, and even worse: my drink is empty. Finally, I hear my drag name called and walk the red carpet as cameras flash and people cheer.

I get to the Sip N Twirl bar and remember the most enticing reason I do this every year: Drag queens drink for free! It's so much fun mingling with the other queens, the sexy, shirtless men and the blue collar Long Island families who are oddly attracted to the event. An invitation to a backyard BBQ leads to an impromptu performance where we wind up in the pool, wigs and all.

At this point, we realize we have missed the ferry back to the Grove, and will soon be those tragic queens stumbling down the beach, heels in hand. As I get back to the Grove and lay my wig in the sun to dry, I remember the most important reason I do this: Because I live in a country where I can.

Carl, Levonia and Paul placing as Miss Sip N Twirl during the 2014 Invasion. Pro-tip: Note the cocktail next to my purse, which I put down so people don't see Levonia with a drink in her hand in every picture.

MISS CHERRY'S

While there are no major drag competitions in July, August heats up with the Miss Cherry's competition, held every year at Cherry's on the Bay. Since you don't have to be a local to enter, drag queens come from all over to compete in the contest. The pageant kicks off around five, but I never go since it takes place during the heart of the summer when the humidity is always like 98 percent, and the sun starts beating directly into the bar at six o'clock during the contest, turning the entire place into a pizza oven.

Drag queens get introduced, walk around in evening wear, do a number, and someone wins. I mean, I would elaborate more, but I can't seem to last more than ten minutes without collapsing from heat exhaustion. Did I mention I have to take salt pills cuz I sweat so much? WHAT THE FUCK AM I DOING ON THIS ISLAND!?!?!?!?

Don't get me wrong. Everyone loves the Miss Cherry's contest and I really don't mean to disparage it. I've just never entered it because I can't do drag in August since it's so fucking hot, so I don't have a fun story to share. But I will profess my love for Cherry's in the next essay, so like *chill the F out, okay?*

THE READING ROOM

One event I did attend at Cherry's religiously was a weekly event hosted by a then-undiscovered Bianca Del Rio on Friday nights. This was years before she went on to win season six of *RuPaul's Drag Race*, starred in two feature films and started touring the world. Back then, Bianca was known for her quick wit and ability to insult just about anyone in the world without them getting offended. I've seen her throw some of the nastiest shade at people, who always leave the stage smiling and laughing. It's an amazing skill.

I think Bianca is able to get away with insulting people because she has such a kind heart and people can sense this when she calls them, "should have been-aborted white trash from Ronkonkoma." Either that, or they can tell that bitch's wit is so quick, they need to get off stage before she calls them out on their face tattoo.

WIG . . . IN A BOX

As a DJ, drag queen and bonafide nightlife enthusiast, I've befriended lots of drag queens over the years. Shape-shifters come in all shapes, sizes, and styles — from campy to fishy, small to large, and everything in between. My obsession with gender identity and cross-dressing began with Divine, who I guess you could say was my gateway drug to drag. When I first laid eyes on her in John Waters's *Pink Flamingos* in tenth grade, I was stunned. I was also in love. A few years later, when I started going to gay bars in NYC, I gravitated to places like Boy Bar and Crow Bar in the East Village that threw parties hosted by cutting-edge drag queens like Linda Simpson, Lahoma Van Zandt and Lady Bunny. Now, I am hashtag blessed to count Lady Bunny, Linda Simpson and a ton of other downtown drag queens as friends.

Although it's fun to dabble in the dark art of drag, there are downsides. While you are just about guaranteed to get attention, sometimes it's not the type you want. An interesting thing a lot of drag queens will tell you is that cross-dressing attracts a lot of men who identify as "straight" but secretly want to sleep with men who dress as women. If you ask me, they're gay AF, but can't come out for whatever reason and need to justify their urge to suck dick by doing it with a guy in pantyhose.

If you ask a lot of drag queens — especially the ones who work in comedy — we don't really look at ourselves sexually. Most of us think of ourselves as clowns. Of course there are pageant queens who see themselves as sex objects and are fine with the kind of attention it attracts. But for the most part, most comedy queens realize they are entertainers in the three-ring circus of gay nightlife.

That's why I always find it odd whenever I'm dressed in drag on Fire Island and some "straight" guy from Long Island hits on me. First of all, I have facial hair. Part of me knows his grandmother in Huntington probably does, too, but still. If he thinks this thing in a leopard-print bikini with a beard and a bulge is a woman, the only person he's deluding is himself. But regardless, countless "straight" men hit on me or try to lure me down the boardwalk to peel my bikini aside so they can go down on me in the bushes.

This repulses me. Sure, it would be hot to get blown by a construction worker — but not in drag. I mean, the last thing I want to do is get a blowjob with heels on. I'm a gay man attracted to other gay men who are into gay men — not the non-binary tragedy known as Levonia Jenkins. And besides, I don't want to be some weirdo freak you use to justify your gayness. Whenever a man hits on me when I'm in drag, my semi-tucked dick shrivels back along my taint even more. There is nothing remotely sexual about having sex in drag to me. I need to have sex as a man.

But some of my cross-dressing friends don't have these issues and enjoy sleeping with men when they're dressed as women. In fact, some of them use it as a lure. Gusty Winds, a drag queen who's performed on Fire Island for years, sometimes pretends to be trans on Craigslist even though she's a full-on man. She says 90 percent of the time, the blue collar men who show up at her door could care less that she painted her face over her five o'clock shadow or that she "drew" breasts on her chest with makeup. She says most of them just want to get fucked by a "woman."

My friend Sherry Vine also hooks up with "straight" men by standing outside the men's room in nightclubs.

"Honey, I've gone down on some of the hottest men in the world wearing this wig!" she once told me.

Sherry has also been known to date "straight" men who discover her when she performs. A lot of them text her for late-night booty calls, and she's more than happy to oblige if she's dressed in drag.

"But whenever I get a text and I'm not in drag, I just tell them I'm out of town. I mean, I'm not gonna get dressed in drag to have sex! I'm not *that* desperate for dick!"

One night, as Sherry was heading home from one of her gigs, she got a text from one of her fuckbuds: "Hey, can my girlfriend and I come over?"

Baffled and a little drunk, she assumed he was trying to ask her to dress him in drag, which she was *not* feeling.

"Honey, I wasn't going to dress up that closet case so we could have sex as girls!"

But after he explained he was with his *actual* girlfriend, Sherry found herself a little nervous, yet aroused.

"I hadn't slept with a woman since high school, and I found the whole thing exciting!"

When they arrived, she thought they would probably just want her to watch the two of them have sex, but instead, he wanted Sherry to fuck him as his girlfriend watched. They started having sex, and a few minutes later, he called his girlfriend over. At this point, he switched positions with Sherry, who in turn started getting pounded from behind. She soon realized her face was now nestled right between his girlfriend's legs.

"He pushed my head down and before I knew it, I was eating her pussy while he fucked me from behind! Performing cunnilingus for the first time, I kept thinking, 'Siri, Mapquest clitoris!' Then, at one point, I had to pull my wig back down on my forehead cuz he was pounding me so hard it practically popped off my head! And there was no way I was going to ruin the illusion and stop riding that dick!" she added.

"Oh, girl," I told her, "There was no illusion in that room that night – we both know it was more of a *de*lusion!"

She laughed and said, "Call it what you want, but it was the hottest three-way I've ever had! You should try it sometime!"

"Thanks," I told her...but I think I'll stick to having this kind of sex in drag . . . "

Some shots from my parody of Madonna's "SEX" book,
shot entirely on Fire Island - available on www.gregscarnici.com
("I'm not the same. I have no shame." – Madonna)

GOOD MORNING!

One of the most popular restaurants in Cherry Grove is a breakfast spot called Floyd's, which is beloved by townsfolk and tourists alike. It's owned and operated by an excitable man named Brett, who named the restaurant after his dog. Floyd's is known for its famous breakfast sandwich, and for having the most consistently good food on the island. Whether you order a farmer's market omelet or the decadent breakfast burrito, you're guaranteed a great start to your day.

Although I love the food at Floyd's, I can never bring myself to go there because I'm the polar opposite of a morning person. I sleep late, don't drink coffee, and the only way I can wake up is by torturing myself in the gym for an hour. After I come home, take a shower and eat, I finally start transitioning from my zombielike state to something that sort of resembles a human being? Before that, I have no interest in seeing other people, let alone being thrust into a hot, sunny area where everyone has been jacked on coffee since 7 AM.

Paul, on the other hand, is the total opposite of me. Venus wakes him up at 5:30 AM every day and he's on his third cup of coffee by the time I wake up three hours later. He loves the morning, while I DO NOT. Since he has no problem getting up early, Paul decided to work at Floyd's one summer when he was in between legal jobs. He had no problem getting up with the sun and working in a hot kitchen all morning long. I, on the other hand, would probably have to pop one of my damn salt pills every fifteen minutes and would still wind up collapsing from heat exhaustion. But Paul loved his time at Floyd's, and continues to visit the restaurant all the time.

The last time I dragged my carcass there, I was ready to murder someone by the time my order arrived. It all began when the sun started beating down on me as I waited to place my order, making me sweat uncontrollably. As my heat stroke started to kick in, all these bright, chipper people kept coming up to vomit whatever story that fucking coffee made them think other people would be remotely interested in hearing from them.

First, a waiter from Cherry's just *had* to tell me how "Tina Burner gagged everyone at her show last night!" Then Lisa Marie, one of the fifty gym teachers on the island, ran up to tell me how "Logan bitched out this wasted girl from Ocean Beach" at a show while her Yorkie barked in my face. *That* joy was followed by someone I barely knew with cuckoo eyes, who felt the need to tell me about the guy he hooked up with the night before while using the words *penis* and *moist*. I wanted to throw up.

I mean, what is wrong with these people? Does caffeine blind them to the fact that some people are not even remotely awake or interested in engaging with the real world until at least noon? And to be honest, even if I was alert, I would have zero interest in hearing any of these stories anyway. But if it's 10 AM and I haven't worked out yet, you can forget about it.

After I finally got to the counter to place my order, I had to deal with the surly man at the register who cuts the heart out of your chest with his eyes if you don't know exactly what you want the second you interact with him. Just a moment's hesitation — which usually comes from the fact that my mind has not remembered how to make words yet — and he snaps, making you feel like some sort of inbred moron.

"What do you *want?*" he snarled at me the last time I was there. Although I showed up knowing just what I was in the mood for, he startled me.

"Uh, I'll have some pancakes and an English Breakfast Tea," I told him.

"How do you want your eggs?" he asked.

"Um . . .over easy?" I asked/told him.

"$14.50. Next!"

By the time he finished taking my money and moved onto the person behind me, I was just about ready to start smoking crack. As I sat there waiting for my pancakes in the dining area by the walkway, I became privy to a non-stop parade of hopped-up, caffeinated people marching through town with their dogs; lesbians on their way to pick up their packages of Dippity Do hair gel or whatever the fuck they had shipped to the post office; lunatics *returning* from Long Island via the ferry they caught at 7:20 AM with carts of food they bought at Costco; and, of course, that methed-out gardener who'd been up since Saturday enthralling me with some story about . . . the cellular structure of plastic? Meth addicts going off on unsolicited questionable scientific tangents like this in casual conversation is always a treat. Especially at 10 AM.

If you've had a few drinks the night before, triple this horror by 3,000 and you'll see why taking a trip downtown for breakfast is not for me. Thankfully, Paul and Carl both drink coffee and are up by 7 AM, so I have no problem paying for everyone's breakfast if either of them will take the seven-minute walk to Floyd's to pick it up for us when I rouse at nine. Then I can devour my breakfast in peace as I scroll through Facebook and secretly judge everyone from the privacy of my own home.

THE HELP

Sadly, business owners have a hard time finding good workers on the island. A lot of people think a summer on Fire Island means a three-month party, and are not prepared for the long, hard hours one must put in as soon as Memorial Day hits. On top of this, seasonal jobs sometimes attract the kind of people who can't hold regular positions because they're ex-cons, raging drunks or drug addicts. While a good interview may get you the job, partying after your shift ends every night of the week just might end with a one-way ticket to Sayville.

Usually, Memorial Day weekend is the litmus test business owners use to figure out if new hires are going to work out. It's sort of trial by fire, as the island gets flooded with thousands of visitors literally overnight. Over the years, I've seen countless bright-eyed workers arrive in April, gung ho to spend the summer on the island who wind up packing their bags by May 31st. While there are lots of stories about waiters and bartenders crashing and burning quickly, a cook was recently hired at one of the restaurants in Cherry Grove who took this to a whole new level.

Over Memorial weekend, a new cook decided to have "a drink" at one of the bars after the kitchen closed. Somewhere around his fourth whiskey soda, a manager saw him stuff a plastic bottle of mayonnaise into his jeans. Outraged, the manager confronted the cook, who tried to defend himself by saying one of the waiters told him he could take it. When the manager asked him to point out which employee told him this, he just stared at him for a long time.

Why this man decided to pocket a bottle of mayonnaise when he had access to gallon drums of it is beyond me. This just had to be some kind of Winona Ryder kind of deal. Anyway you cut it, he was thrown out of the bar and asked not to return. Amazingly, an hour later, he tried to get back into the bar by wrapping a green scarf around his head. The manager walked right up and asked him, "Are you really trying to get back in here wearing a *disguise*?!" and was once again met with silence. The cook then slowly slunk away.

Since the island is so small, word soon got back to the owner of the restaurant about the cook's mangled mayonnaise heist. "Oh, I wouldn't worry about him," she said. "He's not gonna last. He was already put on warning twice." She was right. By the end of the week, he was gone — green scarf and all — and replaced by another drunk who lasted *two* weeks.

ROLL WITH IT

I can't wait to grow up so I can be a seventy-year-old lesbian who drives a jazzy around Cherry Grove. Although motorized vehicles are illegal on the boardwalks without a permit, sometimes I'll go for a run and pass a dozen lesbians riding jazzies and golf carts all over town. I know they probably need knee replacement surgery like every other woman over the age of sixty, which is why I decided I'm going to transition into a female when I get older like Caitlyn Jenner. Then I'll be able to get one of them damn jazzies and run people off the boards, too. And hopefully wind up on the cover of *Vanity Fair*, too.

JEAN NAIVETE

I used to be very naive. In my teens and twenties, I was dimmer than a fifteen-watt bulb and gave everyone the benefit of the doubt. Like an idiot, it never entered my mind that people might have ulterior motives. For this reason, I was burned a lot, and finally started wising up in my thirties. Today, it takes me a while to warm up to people and I'm happy to have a nice, tight circle of friends I call family.

Now that I'm in my forties, cross me just once and you'll get the chop on Facebook and in real life within seconds. I don't have time for assholes or people who try to take advantage of me. But back when I was younger, I suffered fools and found myself in lots of weird situations because besides being as innocent as a mentally challenged kitten, I was also a bonafide freak magnet. People must have seen me coming a mile away the second they saw my bright-eyed smile.

My magnet must have been set to black hole-level proportions the night I seemingly conjured a freak out of thin air while barbecuing in our backyard in Cherry Grove. It was a warm August night, and as I was grilling some chicken, I heard someone calling me from the boardwalk.

"Hey, buddy!" I heard as I looked around wondering who was talking to me. "You think I can use your grill?"

Confused, I walked towards the boardwalk and peered into the night. My eyes adjusted to the darkness and I saw a thin, shirtless man holding a Ziploc bag. From what I could tell, he was in his early 50s, and had that hollowed-out ex- or current meth addict look about him.

"I brought a steak with me this morning and I was hoping to barbecue it," he said. He pointed to a cooler between his legs. "It's been marinating all day and I was hoping I could use your grill?" he said/asked.

Taken aback, I told him I'd be right back. I went to find Paul, who was setting the table for dinner.

"Paul!" I said. "There's a man outside who wants to grill a steak on our barbecue."

"What?" he said. "Who is it? Do you know him?"

"Um, no, he just sort of called to me from the boardwalk?" I told him.

He shot me a look I was familiar with that meant, "What have you gotten into now, dumbass?" and ran to the deck, ready to take action. By the time he got outside, our neighbor John had already beat him to it.

"You need to leave. Now!" John shouted at the weirdo, who was still holding his marinated steak in the Ziploc bag as if it was some kind of prize fish.

"Okay, got it!" the man said. Then he scampered down the boardwalk with his steak and cooler, obviously used to the reaction he was getting.

Paul turned to me. "What is wrong with you? How do these people *find* you?" he asked.

I just shrugged. "I don't know — but I was put on the spot and didn't know what to say," I added.

"Well *I* did," John said. "He needed to leave. I mean who goes up to strangers and asks to use their barbecue? Would *you* ever do that?" he asked.

" . . . No?" I sheepishly responded.

"Exactly," he said. "You need to get a backbone, honey."

As fate would have it, *six years later*, John was sitting on the beach when a man came up to him and started talking about the surf.

After a few minutes, John peered at him and said, "You seem familiar, but I can't place it." Instantly, it came to him and he realized he was talking to the freak with the steak.

"Wait. Did you once ask to use a barbecue so you could grill a steak?" he asked the man, who turned pale. "You need to leave. Now," John told him. Again. And he did.

Since "the steak incident," I've gotten a lot better at reacting to people when I'm put on the spot. Like when I get random messages on Facebook from strangers who want to "come visit me on Fire Island" for the weekend — or better yet — guys who message me on SCRUFF looking for a place to crash when they haven't even sucked my dick yet. Now, I have no problem telling them, "Get to steppin." Sure, I may have fewer "friends" because of this, but at least I'm not grilling steaks for strangers.

TRAPPED

As soon as March hits, friends start dropping hints about coming to visit me on the island. I'll get random texts like, "Are you getting excited for Fire Island?" that make me think, "No, but you are." ●●

By the time May hits, everyone I've ever met starts texting me that they want to come "see me." Listen. I have no problem entertaining friends. In fact, I love it. Most of the people in my life are creative, fun and slightly insane — the perfect recipe for a good time. But sometimes, I'll invite people I don't know so well and come to the realization I've become trapped hosting a monster.

"Where do you *find* these people?" Carl will ask, as a visitor starts wreaking havoc and full-on exhausting everyone within seconds of arriving. Carl has a lot less patience for bullshit than I do. In fact, it's one of the reasons we're such great friends. He has no time for garbage people, and I'm glad he came into our lives that summer when he slowly, but surely, started placing his chair closer to ours every weekend on the beach. Although he will deny this, that's how I remember getting to know him.

Even though Carl sometimes gets mad at me for putting up with bad behavior from our houseguests, I know these people will be added to my ever-growing travel ban, so there's no reason to start a fight with them when I plan on cutting them out of my life as soon as they board the ferry.

On the flipside, some people who come to visit are so heinous; I have no other course of action but to confront them when they reveal themselves to be deranged or horrendous. Sadly, this happened with Matt, a handsome twenty-three-year-old I invited to the island after the two of us met on SCRUFF.

To be fair, I was under the impression that Matt was like 26 or 27 when we first met. He sported a thick beard that aged him a few years and he was able to text without resorting to the use of GIFS all the time. For a while there, I would never consider having sex with someone practically half my age. But after I turned forty-two, it seemed like every guy in his twenties started hitting on me because I was a *daddy*. Since some of them were too hard to resist, I started making exceptions, even though, in my experience, there's a maturity and generational gap that can be hard to bridge with an age difference like that. But when no one's doing much talking, who gives a fuck, right?

Although Matt was born in Long Island, he had never been to Fire Island. Since I have a paternal side from being a fucking *daddy*, I decided to invite him to comes visit so his first experience on Fire Island would be a good one. He was newly out and didn't have a lot of gay friends, and I thought it would be nice to introduce him to NYC's gay summer camp with Paul and Carl. I also knew they'd love him since he was really sweet and would be make the perfect houseguest.

At this point, you may be wondering WTF I'm doing fucking guys like Matt when I'm in a relationship with Paul, so here's a little backstory. Paul and I met back in 1993 while I was in college and he was in law school. We quickly fell in love over frozen margaritas at Bandito's in the West Village and were monogamous for the first five years we were together. After that, we started having three-ways, as a lot of the gays do. A few years later, we felt comfortable enough to open up the relationship so we could meet up with guys on our own. Paul and I have never been jealous and have no problem with this scenari-ho because we're confident in our love for one another. For this reason, Paul has no problem meeting guys I sleep with, like Matt, and I feel the same way about meeting the hideous piece of shit bastards he fucks. LOL JK.

When Matt got to the island, the three of us showed him a great time. We had drinks on our roof deck as the sun set and Paul grilled us dinner. Later that night, we brought Matt to a drag show at Cherry's since he was a huge *RuPaul's Drag Race* fan. When the show ended, we planned on taking him to the Underwear Party at the Ice Palace, but Paul and Carl bowed out because they were tired from long weeks at work.

Matt and I went to the party alone and stripped down to our underwear. We grabbed a drink and I could see he was in awe as he looked around at all the men partying in their skivvies. He was like a kid in a candy store and I instantly ceased to exist as he scanned the room looking at all the hot, shirtless guys. I gave him a tour of the party, showing him the dance floor and introducing him to a few bartenders. Then I brought him by the infamous back room.

Even though the two of us were still having sex, and had not yet morphed into the "we used to hook up, but now we're friends" zone, he showed zero interest in me and quickly darted into the sea of men. I told him I would be by the DJ booth after I grabbed a drink, and he said he'd meet me there in a few minutes. *Half an hour later*, when he still didn't show up, I went to find him. I walked into the back room and saw him coming right towards me.

"I'm going home," I told him.

He quickly responded, "I know how to get home. I'll see you tomorrow."

I was at a loss for words. Did this insolent kid really plan on abandoning his host so he could suck off strangers in the back room of an underwear party? Instead of confronting him, I simply gave him one of my patented death glances, turned, and walked away. A few minutes later, as I was getting dressed on the outside deck, I turned to see him right behind me.

"I'll go home with you," he said.

"Do whatever you want," I told him. "I was just done hanging out by myself."

"You're clearly mad, so I'm gonna go home with you," he replied.

"Fine," I said.

On the way home, I tried to explain why his actions were rude. I told him if we were with a bunch of friends and he disappeared for half an hour, it would have been fine, but since it was just the two of us, it wasn't right to leave me on my own so he could have sex with randos. You know, the classic "bros before hos" kind of deal.

He told me he had never experiences anything like the back room before and that he got "caught up." Then he started backtracking by making excuses and saying ridiculous things like, "But I'll never get a chance to come to Fire Island ever again."

Finally, I reached the point where I'd had enough. "Either you understand why it was rude to leave me alone or you don't. I mean I'm accepting your apology and then you start taking it all back by trying to defend yourself."

"I'm trying to *explain* myself," he nastily replied. "This is Fire Island! I got caught up, all right?!"

It was then I realized the gin he was drinking was making him ornery.

"Okay, fine. Now let's hug this out and go back to the house so we can leave this in the past," I told him.

He replied by staring at me with an evil look that rivaled the one I gave him at the Ice Palace. "I don't want to be touched by you right now," he said as he crossed his arms.

I was aghast. And officially done. I started walking home.

On the way back to the house, he kept arguing with me, totally negating his apology and making me even more enraged. At this point, I realized he was either a bad drunk, a complete lunatic, twenty-three years old, or — most likely — all three. Still, I set up his bed and wished him a good night. His replied with a threat that he would be leaving in the morning.

Thank fucking God, I thought.

The next day, Matt woke up before I did and had coffee with Paul and Carl. After the two of them hit the beach, Matt sauntered into my room and sat on the bed. He was acting kind of sheepish and sad, and I realized he must have given some thought to what happened the night before and was trying to make amends. I accepted his apology, gave him a hug and we moved on.

Or so I thought.

We wound up having an amazing Saturday — spending the afternoon on the beach, getting drunk while I DJed a tea dance, seeing a short film of mine that was playing in a festival, and celebrating by dancing at Cherry's afterwards. Since the two of us were out late the night before, I decided to head home around one. I told Matt he could stay out dancing with Paul and Carl, but he said he was tired and wanted to go home, too.

On the way back to the house, he started rehashing the events of the night before.

"I thought we were done with this," I said.

But he wouldn't let it go. He became argumentative and started making up more excuses. I once again realized all those gin and tonics weres turning him more aggressive than a 'roided-out circuit queen in Mykonos and chose not to engage with him, which further set him off.

When we got to the house, the last words I whispered before heading to bed were, "You know, you're *sick and sadistic*! There's something wrong with you!"

Looking back, I realize I sounded like Krystle Carrington on *Dynasty*, but at the time, it completely captured how I felt. Besides, if you can't pull a bitchy diva moment on Fire Island, where can you? And, clearly there was something wrong with this person.

For the second night in a row, we went to bed mad at one other. In the morning, he got up early and had coffee with Paul and Carl as I slept in. The three of them hit the beach, but I stayed in bed late cuz I'm a gimp who has to get eight hours of sleep, otherwise I get sick. (More on this in my next book, *I Was Born a Gimp*.)

When Matt came back to the house, I got back into Krystle Carrington mode and told him he really was sick and sadistic. He told me he was an anxious person who thought about things a lot and sometimes became obsessive. I told him that was fine, but that I thought he either had a drinking problem or shouldn't have gin because he became belligerent. He left in tears on the next ferry and I added another person to my ban list.

The next day, Matt texted me a long-winded apology saying he felt horrible for ruining my weekend and making me feel uncomfortable in my own home. He ended by saying he hoped I would talk to him when my feelings settled down. I told him I needed space, but in my mind, I was done. I told him how I had tons of great friends and never fought with anyone, so why would I want to continue a new friendship that was bringing me so much discord? Throughout the week, he sent more texts, explaining how our falling-out had depressed him and how he hoped I would talk to him.

I acquiesced, and he explained that his way of working through problems was by talking about them ad nauseam. He said he cared for our friendship and felt terrible about everything that had happened. I chose to give him a second chance and he turned out to be one of those rare people who actually *do* change. Since "the incident," the two of us have grown very close. I've even embraced my Daddyness by becoming a father figure to him, and I enjoy helping him navigate adulthood and all the challenges it brings. I've also become his drag-mother. In 2018, he started having a bigger interest in drag and I started giving him makeup, brushes and advice about performing. Like many gay relationships that start by hooking up, Matt and I no longer sleep together and now love each other as friends.

I just don't let that asshole drink gin when we go out.

THE BIPOLAR EXPRESS

Although Matt's visit still conjures up memories only rivaled by the time my bipolar cousin came to visit when her lithium wasn't working, both those trips seem downright peaceful to the time Lance, another SCRUFF trick I became friends with, came to stay with us one weekend. (*Note to self:* Stop inviting guys you meet on SCRUFF to Fire Island.)

I quickly bonded with Lance after we hooked up one afternoon in Brooklyn. The two of us had been messaging for months and I was excited to finally meet him. He was hairy, bearded and had a classically handsome Greek face. When he showed up at my apartment, I was pleasantly surprised to find out he was even more attractive in person. The sex was great, and afterwards, we got to know each other as we talked in bed for an hour, laughing easily.

After we showered, he invited me to go to Austin, Texas with him for a design project he was working on. In one of the worst decisions of my life, I decided to go. In my defense, it was the week of SXSW, and I knew I had friends working on the festival I could stay with if things got weird.

Not so shockingly, the trip wound up being as disastrous as you might imagine. While on the plane there, he drunkenly revealed he was really an escort and the hotel room we were staying in was being paid for by one of his clients. The next four days were filled with just about everything you'd think would follow a confession of this nature at 39,000 feet in the air by someone you've only known for twenty-eight hours.

Although we drifted apart after that disastrous trip, we saw one other every once in a while when Lance came to New York for escort work, and he proved to be alternatingly insane-fun and insane-draining. There was always some kind of drama in his life. He was constantly losing his wallet, having fights with friends, moving to different cities — whenever I spoke to him, his life was in chaos.

A year after we met, things seemed like they were finally settling down. He met a nice guy in Vancouver and they moved in together. A few months later, he came to New York City to buy his fianc-gay an engagement ring and stayed with us in Brooklyn. The fact that he was buying an engagement ring after being with his boyfriend for three months was a total red flag, but the weekend was so drama-free, Paul and I didn't think twice when he asked if he could visit us on the island that summer. Needless to say, this wound up being a bigger mistake than going on vacation with someone you've only known for twenty-eight hours.

I picked up Lance at the ferry one Thursday in June. The exhaustion started the second he saw me all sweaty from a run.

"Ew! You're disgusting! Don't touch me!" he said, a greeting that already had me wishing I hadn't told him to come out. "I'm *starving*! I've been up since six and I need to eat something *now!*" he announced.

I took him to the deli and he ordered a chicken sandwich. He brought it back to the house, and as I was pulling off my drenched tank top on the deck, I heard him complaining from inside.

"This chicken is gross! And the bread is *disgusting!*" he screamed.

I just ignored him. "I'm gonna take a shower," I said as I headed into the bathroom.

As soon as I got out of the bathroom, he was three inches from my face. "I want to have a photo shoot! I need new pictures for my Rentmen.com ad. And I need to work out! I got so fat! Oh! We got a dog! He's so cute! I love him! Hey, what are we doing for dinner? When is Paul getting here? I want to do drag this weekend!" he stream-of-consciousness spewed at me as I got dressed.

After I finally slipped on some shorts, I headed into the kitchen to make a sandwich.

"Make one for me, too! I'm hungry! I need to eat! I want to put on muscle!" he announced.

Huh? He just told me he got fat and now he wanted two lunches in twenty minutes? Nothing made sense with this one. I was already exhausted and he had only been here an hour. While we were eating, he checked his phone.

"Oh, great, I came to New York to get clients, and now that I'm on Fire Island, they're messaging me from the city! I need to make money on this trip! It's why I came here!" he complained. "Wait! Put your phone down! Check out the new website I created for my art directing career!" he oddly tossed in.

When we were done eating, I told him I was heading to The Pines to help a friend move some furniture.

"We're not walking, are we? We need to take a water taxi!" he announced.

"Um . . . it's a fifteen-minute walk and I thought you said you wanted to get exercise?" I said.

"Okay, I'll walk, but it better not take forever!" he replied.

After we were done helping my friend, Lance wanted to check out the general store in The Pines. Although he was just complaining about needing money, he dropped one hundred dollars on *two candles* and I had to talk him out of buying a $500 pair of sunglasses. Afterwards, we went food shopping for dinner, which — thanks to his manic shopping style — wound up costing $120. When we were done, we headed back to The Grove to relax. Or so I thought.

As soon as we got to the house, he started tearing into my drag closet. "I want to have a photo shoot!" he demanded.

"Okay," I told him. "I just need to go see my neighbor and I'll be back soon."

The truth was that I needed some time away from him. When I

returned half an hour later, he was in full drag.

"Come on! You have to get dressed! It's time for the photo shoot!" he demanded. Although I thought I would just be shooting him in drag, I figured I'd wind up with a few pictures I could throw on Instagram and decided to get dressed, too.

We headed to my roof and shockingly had a fun time. While we were shooting on his iPhone, he got a notification.

"I got a client in The Pines!" he announced.

I was thrilled. "Great! When? Where? For how long!?!" I enthusiastically asked, matching his manic energy.

He told me he set up the date for 9 PM, so the two of us had a quick dinner before he headed into the night.

"Sorry I can't clean up — I have to clean out!" he said, which made me want to throw up.

When we woke the next day, he realized he left his watch at his client's house and had to go back to get it.

"Oh, shucks!" I said. "But we can hang out when you get home."

"Sure thing!" he told me.

I decided to get some writing done while he was gone, even though I kept getting texts from him every ten seconds.

"Where are you?"

"What are you doing?"

"What are we doing for lunch?"

I told him to pick something up at the grocery store and that I'd pay him back. A few hours later, he came home and announced he was grilling up salmon for lunch. I told him that was great, since I was working on a story and just needed another half an hour to finish it up. As I continued trying to write, he kept screaming at me from the kitchen.

"Come in here! Pick the yellow leaves off this cilantro! Make some lemon zest! Can you turn the barbecue on? Open up some rosé!"

I closed my laptop and realized I would *not* be getting any work done.

After we finished eating, I paid Lance a compliment by saying what a good cook he was.

"I know, but I don't want to do it for a living! I want to start a YouTube series! You can shoot the videos and edit them and then I'll have an Instagram account where I post pictures of my meals and then I'll put out a few cookbooks!" he announced.

That settled it. He was deranged.

When he was done redirecting the course of our lives for the next year, he decided it was time for another photo shoot. He went to take a shower, as I cleaned up the kitchen and started doing dinner prep. Ten minutes later, he marched out of the bathroom completely naked and ran over to me in the kitchen.

"What are you doing?! We're having a photo shoot!" he screamed.

I started to crack.

"I was starting to work on dinner while you were in the shower. Besides, you're not even dressed!" I said.

"I know! I need you to get your early '80s athletic wear out for the shoot!"

I was done. I threw the dishes in the sink and grudgingly helped dress/pose/shoot him so he could update his pictures on Rentmen.com to get more "high-end clients" in his tacky Nasty Pig fucking jockstrap.

"No! Go lower! A little further back! I want you to show more of my body!" he announced.

I was purposely trying to crop his fat gut out of the shot so he'd look better, but after he kept being so demanding, I just did whatever the fuck he wanted in the hopes the goddamn photo shoot would end. When it finally did, I was done.

"We need to talk," I said. "You are completely exhausting. From the second you got here, you've been demanding I do things for you and I feel like I'm in fifth grade being bullied! I don't like feeling this way. This is not how people treat one another!" I told him.

His face dropped. "I've heard this before." (Red Flag #38.) "But I'm glad you consider me a good enough friend to tell me. I'll try to be more aware of this. I was just really excited to be here."

Bitch, please, I thought. This person was obviously bipolar and I was lucky enough to get him during one of his manic phases. He tried to win me back by kissing me. I mean, did he really think he was going to fix things with some cheap whore trick? At this point, I was less attracted to him than Matt after he told me he didn't want to be touched.

Thankfully, Paul showed up with our friend Michael a few hours later. Over the course of the weekend, Lance switched his attention to them, and every time he demanded I do something like come see how he Photoshopped his fat gut in one of the pictures I took of him, he'd catch himself and say, "Whenever you have time! Not this second, though!" Somehow, that made it even worse.

All weekend long, Lance kept bragging about what an amazing escort he was and how much money his clients paid him. When Paul started rolling his eyes every time he opened his mouth, I knew he had had enough, too. When Paul told us he had to go stake tomato plants in the garden, I knew he was lying to get away from Lance because he did that the weekend before. His ruse worked and Michael and I were stuck with him.

Lance turned his attention to Michael. "We have to go to the store! I'm cooking dinner tonight and I need to buy some ingredients!" he announced.

After an hour of listening to him whine, Michael finally decided to go shopping with him. Ten minutes later, I got a text: "He's buying everything in the store! The bill came to $170! He's been darting around the store like Pac-Man!"

When they got back to the house, Lance started badgering Michael to help him make the marinade for the chicken. When that was done, he started bullying him to get into drag so the two of them could come to the tea dance I was DJing dressed up. An hour later, while I was spinning at the Tiki Bar, Lance had the *nerve* to show up wearing a new pair of heels I bought *just that week.*

"I'm breaking them in for you!" he said when I confronted him for wearing them. Ugh. He was the *worst.*

Lance stayed at the party thirty minutes before demanding Michael go back to the house for a costume change.

"Girl, I just got here and am not heading back to the house to change. Besides, I look amazing," Michael told him.

Lance kept bothering him to leave until Michael finally snapped.

"I'm staying here," he said as he turned his back to Lance. Thirty minutes later, Lance showed up in another look, hoping to get even more attention from the strangers who were boring him so much he had to leave just an hour ago.

Here's a thing I've come to discover about escorts: Many of them are demanding, needy, don't understand boundaries and are *exhausting.* A winning combination. With Lance, simple things like not being able to find his watch turn into dramatic events. On top of that, he was randomly whipping his dick out and trying to make out with everyone. It was bizarre. So when he told us he got a client back in the city and would be leaving on the 2 PM ferry the next day, we were thrilled.

The second he left, Michael turned to us. "My God, I feel like I just took an Adderall. That guy is *a lot,*" he said.

"Do you know when I helped him by grilling the chicken last night when he was having that meltdown about his watch, he told me I could have cooked it a little longer? Can you imagine?" Paul said. "Did any of us get salmonella? I don't think so!"

"Thank fucking God he's gone!" I said as I reached for the vodka to make us some much-needed Bloody Marys. Then I added Lance to my travel ban. For life.

DO'S AND DON'TS ON BEING
A HOUSEGUEST ON FIRE ISLAND

Needless to say, after these encounters, and various others — including the time my bipolar cousin screamed at her boyfriend for thirty minutes on our roof deck at 11:30 PM for all of Fire Island to hear — I decided to write the following essay, featuring a few do's and don'ts on being a houseguest on Fire Island.

One of the best (and worst) parts of having a summer home is being able to invite guests to visit. Some guests are great, and jump to help with any task, while others just sit around all weekend, waiting for you to serve them breakfast, lunch and dinner. Since I work in comedy and nightlife, I've had a lot of houseguests which include a plethora of DJs, drag queens, go-go boys, burlesque dancers and even a day trader or two (don't ask). If you're wondering why some get the honor of returning to sleep on the slow-leaking blow-up mattress in the living room while others do not, I've compiled a few do's and don'ts on being a houseguest on Fire Island.

You're a gay man. Don't text me, "What should I bring!?!?" from Penn Station. Pick up some wine, vodka, tequila . . . anything. Or, if you're coming to the island to visit a sober house — Parcheesi. If you're visiting The Grove, a half-drunk plastic bottle of Georgi *could* suffice, although if you show up with that mess in The Pines, you will immediately be added to the ban list. So bring a bottle of Tito's, or even better, Estée Lauder facemasks.

You're dying to go to tea, but since I live here all summer, I sometimes need a break from watching everyone drink their facelifts off. Go and have a blast! And when I tell you dinner is at ten, please don't text me, "COMING NOW!" at eleven. I may like to cook, but I'm not open 24/7 like some of the bottoms out here.

Speaking of dinner, don't wait until you arrive to inform me you are a gluten-free, lactose intolerant, raw vegan. I have to prepare in advance for that kind of high-maintenance faggotry, and the only thing raw this island serves up is dick. (Speaking of which, don't forget your Truvada.)

So you've devoured that dinner I worked on while you were social-climbing at tea. Now is *not* the time to recline on the couch to check your Instagram notifications. I mean, it's not like anyone is going to like your blurry picture of the sunset anyway, so help clear the table or do the dishes. Or, if you're staying in The Pines, text Esmerelda to have her load the dishwasher and put the Special K in the oven.

Midnight rolls around and we decide to hit the Underwear Party. It's going to be packed, so I tell you to map your way back to the house in case we get separated. But, come 4 AM, my phone starts buzzing incessantly because you're lost and crying outside The Belvedere Guest House. If you're staying in The Pines, just text Esmerelda to bring the yacht over when you're ready to go home.

You finally crash on the blow-up mattress I inflated while you were checking your SCRUFF messages on the couch the night before. Please don't sleep til 2 PM and throw my housemates shade as we creep around you at 10 AM. Or if you're in The Pines, feel free to sleep all day in the air-conditioned pool house they've arranged for you.

Wait a minute — I look closer and see you brought trade home with you? And he's an un-vetted go-go boy from Patchogue? Please don't bring hookups into the house, unless, of course, I introduced you to him. If you find yourself in this situation in The Pines, just throw him $250 to bottom for the house and all will be forgiven.

It's now 3 PM and Sleeping Beauty has finally roused from her slumber and . . . is off to the Ice Palace to see Logan Hardcore's drag show? How about deflating that air mattress first? Or, if you're in The Pines, now is the time to start complimenting Julio on his calf implants to make up for that failed joke about his Botox at high tea the night before.

Sure, a little hair of the dog is always a good idea after you've drunk more than a drag queen hosting bingo, but don't be finishing all the vodka you *didn't* bring and start going through my drag closet! I paid $14.99 for that camouflage jumpsuit and don't need you stretching it out! Actually, if you stay with me, you always have free reign to get into drag. After all, a good carry is always a way to ensure you'll be invited back.

In short, Fire Island can be a wild time. Just be sure you don't act like an animal when you come to visit, or you might just be added to my ever-growing travel ban list.

Me with Logan Hardcore at The Ice Palace
before one of her pool shows, back when I had hair.

HI, GENE!

The odd thing about living on an island all summer long is that sometimes I wind up taking four showers a day, while other times, I realize I haven't showered in like a week. Don't get me wrong, I'm not a dirtbag. I go swimming in the ocean . . . sometimes.

My pits were riper than a black banana when this picture was taken.

GOD IS A DJ

An angel descended from the heavens and appeared before me. Weaving her hands to and fro, she lured me closer and closer as she cast her magical spell. Twirling fingers beckoned me through smoke and swirling lights. Her eyes penetrated the darkness — and my soul. I was in a feverish trance and no longer knew where I ended and she began.

Man was I high.

"Watch over the fried piker. The fuzzy hitch is lazy," I heard from nowhere.

"Huh?" I asked the darkness.

Someone pulled me close. "I said, watch out for the Pied Piper. That fucking bitch is crazy."

I stared at this mysterious figure, trying to sort out who and what it is.

"Come on, we're taking a break," it said. It led me off the dance floor, shoved a bottle of water in my hand and said, "Drink this. Now." I followed its orders and realized I was thirsty beyond belief. What time was it? How long was I dancing for? Was it day or night?

The water cooled me down, and I floated back to reality.

"Greg, are you alright?"

I turned to the voice and began to realize it was coming from the mouth of my friend, Kevin. Oh, so *that's* who this was.

The bastard! For the first time in my history of taking ecstasy, it had worked. And now he was trying to ruin it by making me drink water? What kind of friend was he? I would kill him if I didn't love him so much.

"That girl's a whack job. I call her Crackzilla because she's always cracked out of her mind. She gets her thrills by fucking with people when they're high." And here I thought an angel had come to guide me through the night.

As my eyes came back into focus, I realized where I was — in the lounge of Body & Soul in downtown NYC. There was no mistaking this place, as it was decorated in that factory break room decor which always made one feel like luxuriating: wooden couches covered in the same industrial-grade carpeting as the floor, metal folding chairs and whatever paint they found in the bargain bin at Home Depot slapped on the walls. But nobody went to Body & Soul for the glamour. They went there to get down. So why spend a fortune turning it into something out of *Wallpaper* magazine if everyone was just going to show up in sweatpants?

It was my kind of club. There was no attitude, people came to dance, and the music was amazing. You weren't going to get any "Now That's What I Call Dance Vol. 16!" crap here — just pure, soulful house and disco classics. On its best nights, going to Body & Soul was like attending a block party in Bed Stuy — minus the merry-go-round.

I take that back. If the drugs were good, you *were* on a merry-go-round. Or one of those throw-up rides. It just depended on how good the shit was.

In my experience, no ecstasy trip was the same. Sometimes I'd drop a hit only to turn fetal in the corner as the rest of my friends found God on the dance floor. Other times, it turned out to be pure speed, and I'd wind up chomping on gum and smoking a pack of cigarettes, feverishly talking to strangers between drags. "And then in fifth grade…" I'd go on.

But inevitably, it always came back to my third grade teacher, Mrs. Kuznitz. That aptly named beast tortured me for an entire year because I didn't hold my pencil "right." Every day I was singled out because I didn't hold the pencil "like everyone else." Well guess, what, Mrs. Cunt-tits? I still hold my pencil wrong, as if I'm a two-year-old stabbing a piece of chicken with a fork for the first time. Unlike David Wentworth, who held his pencil "right" and is currently in jail.

As you can see, sometimes I'd go down a very dark spiral. But this time, I'd gotten the real deal.

"Wow, this stuff is great," I told Kevin as I slammed down another bottle of water.

"You're right. This is nothing like that time on Fire Island." Jeez, why did he have to bring that up? This guy was turning out to be a real buzzkill.

(Insert dreamy flashback sound effect . . .)

A few years back, the two of us rented a house in Cherry Grove for a week in August. For some odd reason, we both had jobs that year and were able to afford an oceanfront house instead of that musty, old shack by the bay we usually rented. While laying on the beach one afternoon, Kevin told me his friend Kyle was coming to visit that night, along with Kyle's boyfriend, Sam, and their ecstasy dealer, Joy.

Now maybe it's the way I was raised, but I always bring something when I go to someone's house. Whether it's a bottle of wine or a magnum of vodka, I never show up empty-handed. Especially if I'm bringing friends.

But not Kyle.

When he marched through our door later that day, he handed me a half-eaten bag of salt-and-vinegar potato chips and said, "Thanks for having us. We weren't planning on opening them, but that ferry ride was soooooo long."

Hmmm. The last time I checked, it was *twenty minutes long.*

But these people looked like they traveled to all ends of the earth, instead of on the Long Island Railroad and the ferry like the rest of us. Kyle had bags under his eyes and smelled like Camembert cheese. Kevin said it was because he was "earthy," but after spending a few days with him, I think "depraved" was a much better description.

His boyfriend Sam was a hairdresser who was currently sporting a zebra mohawk and matching sarong. He was bubbly and effervescent, and I actually loved having him around. He had a bright smile on his face the entire visit and always seemed like he was having a great time.

The un-aptly named, Joy, on the other hand, was a mother of two who looked like the Zuni fetish doll from *Trilogy of Terror*. She had a mouthful of jagged, toasted pignoli-nut teeth and wore what appeared to be a large woven basket of hair atop her head. To make her even more endearing, every once in a while she'd let out a cackle that made me want to throw her in the oven. Although she was friendly, you could instantly tell she was insincere, which turned me off the second I met her.

I never would have let these degenerates into our home, but since they had drugs, Kevin welcomed them with open arms. Another flag went up when Kyle started making cocktails for everyone with the liquor *I* schlepped on the island. Filling six pint glasses with gin and topping them off with a twist of lime, he announced, "This drink is gonna be just like heaven. I am sooooo looking forward to a relaxing week."

Come again?

Not one to let things slide, I pulled Kevin aside and asked him what was going on.

"Oh, it must have been a slip. He's gotta manage the restaurant tomorrow night. They're leaving in the morning." Or a few mornings after that, as it turned out.

"We have more gin, right?" Kyle asked as he topped off his drink with the last of the Bombay ten minutes later.

In another four hours, they had polished off the rum and were working through the vodka.

"Anyone want a drink?" Kyle asked, always the host. I guess he thought no one would remember he'd been using all of our liquor if he served them until they passed out. Now I've never been one to mask the way I feel about people, and Kyle must have caught on, as most bottom-feeders do. Although they seem to be clueless, they know just what they're doing. So, as he handed me a vodka cranberry with a fucking *umbrella*, he told me he planned on going to the liquor store in the morning.

"I'd go tonight, but that trip just *wiped me out*."

For someone who was wiped out, he certainly had a lot of energy. While Kevin and I cooked dinner, he insisted on scanning the beach for table garnish.

"A proper dinner is never complete without table garnish," he announced as he threw a pinecone on my plate.

Dinner consisted of four magnums of pinot grigio and a forkful of salmon, as he and his friends were on Atkins (read: alcoholics.) After their "meal" came to an end around the time the rest of us started our salads, Joy announced she was handing out treats to anyone who wanted them.

Hmm, so maybe these people weren't dirtbags after all. If a hit of ecstasy was twenty-five dollars, then four of them would make a very nice hostess gift. In that case, I could put up with a depleted liquor cabinet and these lowlifes.

"That'll be twenty five dollars," she said as she slipped the pill into my hand.

As usual, all the ecstasy did was make me sit in the corner, rocking back and forth with my hands around my knees. But not the rest of the house. Everyone was rocking out to the *Body & Soul Vol. 3* compilation I put on. At 2 AM, I headed to the deck as I waited for the drugs to kick in. At one point, Joy saw me cowering on the chaise lounge and came over to comfort me.

"You just need to get in there and let it do its thing. You'll be feeling great in no time." Two hours later, I was still on that chaise lounge, watching Kyle as he polished off the last of the vodka with a round of kamikaze shots.

Before he finished our entire supply, I decided to make a break for the kitchen to hide the tequila, which he hadn't spied yet. There was no way I was going to let this skeeze finish off all our booze only to sneak away on the ten o'clock ferry! I found the tequila and snuck off to bed with two bottles weighing down my cargo pants. As I said goodnight to my friends, I noticed everyone was in the process of taking another hit.

"That'll be twenty five dollars," Joy said brightly.

I crawled down to the lower level to try and fall asleep. Since the ecstasy never hit me, I figured I'd be out in no time. What I didn't expect was their dance party to rock on until eleven in the morning. At one point, I honestly thought they led a circus elephant into the house and were having it do parlor tricks. The ceiling creaked and bellowed as dust and wood shavings floated around my sleepless body.

At 10 AM, I marched upstairs to find out what was going on. I blinked twice and saw Kyle in the middle of a tribal dance in the living room, jumping up and down to "I Ran So Far Away." I wish I had run away. Visions of *The Exorcist* popped into my mind as I watched his arms flailing about his head, which was rolling back and forth. If this is what a good ecstasy trip was like, I'm glad I never had one. Over on the couch, Sam and Joy were having cocktails. Now, what kind of cocktail could they possibly have concocted? I sauntered over to the kitchen, where I found a bottle of triple sec and three limes laying on the counter.

'Want a margarita?" Kyle asked as he took a break from his epileptic fit to play hostess once again.

"It's 11 AM," I told him. "Is it?" he announced as he threw a splash of Triple Sec and squeezed a lime into a glass. "I had no idea." He took a sip from his "drink" and said, "Mmm. You sure?" I got acid reflux just looking at that concoction and went back to bed.

Five hours later, I awoke to find the entire house empty. I headed to the deck, where I saw Kyle and Sam playing pro kadima on the beach. I looked in the living room and saw that 9,000 seashells had been converted into ashtrays and every single surface was covered with half-filled glasses. Still a little tweaked from the night before, I decided to clean the house.

Thankfully, Kevin and the rest of the house had passed out. They slept the whole day, leaving me in peace after I emptied the dishwasher for the fifth time. I headed to the beach to take a nap as they roused from their slumber just as the sun started to set. I laid my blanket down and listened as the waves lulled me to sleep . . .

"Hey, you find a ring?" someone shrieked at me as I started to drift off.

"What?" I said. "A ring. I was out here early this morning and I lost my ring."

I looked up to see a giant woman with bright red hair towering over me.

"I'm so effin pissed I lost it," she said as she got down on her hands and knees and started sifting through the sand. "I loved that ring. My best friend gave it to me."

"Well, what makes you think you lost it here?" I asked.

"Well, I was partying with two guys on the beach here this morning. Things got real hot and heavy and my ring must have slipped off while we were having sex."

Insert record scratch.

So this woman had sex with Kyle and Sam? Jesus. If a good ecstasy trip meant having sex with a woman when you were gay, I'd much rather be whimpering in the corner obsessing over Mrs. Kuznitz.

"Let me know if you find it. I'm staying at the Ice Palace," she announced as she marched off down the beach.

(Insert dreamy reverse flashback sound effect . . .)

"Come on, let's get back on the dance floor," Kevin said, snapping his fingers to bring me back to reality at Body & Soul, and out of my Fire Island memory wormhole.

"Wow. How long was I zonked out for?"

"Honey, you've been zonked the whole night, but that's not gonna stop us from tearing up that dance floor. Come on, they're playing Shalamar!"

IT'S ECSTASY WHEN YOU LAY DOWN NEXT TO ME

For some reason, my friend Alex always used to put on a *crushed-velvet Austin Powers costume* whenever we dropped ecstasy in the '90s, so you can imagine my surprise when he came to visit us on Fire Island and burst out of the bathroom wearing that purple mess of a suit and offered us a hit of molly, *eighteen years later.*

HEY, MR. DJ

Some people were raised on formula. I was raised on disco.

Born in 1972, my first exposures to music were the pulsating sounds of Donna Summer, the funky beats of Musique and the tongue-in-cheek hits of the Village People. Disco started gaining popularity around 1976, and by 1978, it was everywhere. For that reason, it had a major influence on my taste in music and made me crave the dance floor before I could practically even walk. My older sisters loved disco, too, and every Saturday night, we'd listen to Donna Summer's "Bad Girls" as we waited for *Dance Fever* and *Solid Gold* to come on TV. Some of the boys in my neighborhood may have rocked out to Led Zeppelin or Black Sabbath, but most Saturday nights you could find me lip-synching to Evelyn "Champagne" King or Patrice Rushen in my bedroom.

Although *Dance Fever* and *Solid Gold* showcased pop, they also featured disco and R&B. Except when Deney Terrio, the host of *Dance Fever* would introduce a couple who'd perform a *square dance routine* — or even worse — *polka*. You can imagine the contempt this nine-year-old gaylord felt when he saw some hideous couple from the Midwest dancing to polka when they should have been dancing to Sylvester. But most of the time, *Dance Fever* featured couples dancing to the disco hits of the day: "Turn The Beat Around," "If I Can't Have You," "More Than A Woman" — all the classics Alexa would one day play when you asked that idiot assistant, "Alexa . . . play disco."

My sister, Diane and I would try to copy their dance routines as our older sister, Christine, sat on the couch, hoping one of us would leave our paneled basement to fetch her a snack. Without fail, the second I'd dart upstairs to use the bathroom or answer the phone, "Going My Way?" — as we called her — would ask me to fry her up a plate of macaroni, or better yet, make her a snack plate. I secretly loved making her snack plates, which were made by tossing whatever I could find in the refrigerator on a plate. Pickles, slices of American cheese on top of Ritz crackers, the occasional pepperoncini or marinated mushroom — my snack plates were pretty damn good for an eight-year-old. In fact, I've had worse antipasto platters at weddings in Jersey.

After *Dance Fever* crowned a winner, we'd switch over to *Solid Gold*, which featured gorgeous dancers performing choreographed routines to the hits of the day. My favorite was Darcel, who had Crystal Gayle-length hair and always stole the attention from the other basic bitches around her. I secretly wanted to be Darcel, pretending, that I, too, had a long mane of hair cascading to the floor as I danced to "Hot Stuff" in my bedroom.

Years later, I came across a Wikipedia entry that called the *Solid Gold* dance routines "tasteless" and "bordering on parody." Blasphemy! They were the epitome of class! Even if part of me knew dancers gyrating in animal-print leotards to Kim Carne's "Bette Davis Eyes" made absolutely no sense. Who was I to argue when Darcel was inspiring me to learn "the snake"?

My musical taste was also forged listening to my favorite radio stations: WKTU, KISS FM, and WBLS. It's no shock diversity came naturally to me, since I was only exposed to RNB singers with braids since birth. Whether it was Evelyn "Champagne" King, Sylvester, Stevie Wonder, or Rick James, it seemed all my musical icons had braids. The only exception was the aforementioned Crystal Gayle, who used to stop me from crying when I was a baby whenever she came on TV. My mother told me I would shut up and just stare at the TV whenever she came on . . .

no doubt trying to figure out if her hair was synthetic or human.

As I got older, disco fell out of style, but not for me. KISS and WBLS continued playing disco and R&B, and eventually house and freestyle. Summer evenings revolved around making sure I was tuned to KISS FM for *The Mix at Six*, a radio show that featured disco, R&B, house, hip-hop and freestyle. It was during one of those mixes I first heard a scandalous song called "Another Man" by Barbara Mason.

"Another Man" is easily the most homophobic song ever released. It's about a woman who believes her boyfriend is gay and features a spoken word bridge where she calls him out for being a closet case for like three minutes straight. It includes offensive lyrics like, "And I passed him on the steps one day and he was switching more than I was!" and "There must have been, I figured, a defect . . . of not when he was created, but somewhere down the line something went *wrong*!"

As a secretly gay ten-year-old, I didn't know there was anything wrong with these lyrics — I was just thrilled there was a song on the radio that spoke about being gay. It captivated me even more than Darcel's hair and I'd wait for it to come on every night so I could sing along as she sang, "Another man is beating my time . . .another man is . . . *loving* mine!"

Looking back, it's obvious one of the reasons I was attracted to disco was because of its gay subtext. Flamboyant singers like Sylvester, Jermaine Stewart and Luther Vandross called me to the dance floor and disco divas like Diana Ross and Donna Summer kept me there. As I grew older and started reading books about disco, I realized what I was connecting to was an intrinsic part of the scene.

Although I had lots of interests as a child (dressing like Wonder Woman, playing with my sister's doll that had hair you could make blond or brunette by twisting her scalp around and . . . *Star Wars?*) I knew there were three things I wanted to be when I grew up: a DJ, a remixer and Darcel. Little did I know all these dreams would one day come true on Fire Island. Darcel was the easiest, as all it took was a thirty-dollar wig and a gold lamé leotard. Being a remixer was not as simple, especially since my only experience was making mixes with two tape decks as I created looped versions of the choruses in Freeeze's "I.O.U." and Shannon's "Let The Music Play" when I was a teenager. My earliest trials at DJing were pretty bad, too. I couldn't afford pitch-adjustable turntables and grew frustrated since I couldn't beat match to save my life. My earliest mixtapes were a mess, and I gave up on my dream of becoming a DJ when I got to college.

All of this changed when my friend Nashom came to visit me in Cherry Grove in 2012. While we were hanging out, he told me he recently started DJing on his iPad when he played at The Cock in the East Village. Intrigued, I asked him to show me what app he used. Within an hour, he taught me how to load tracks, set up cue points and mix songs. My first attempts weren't perfectly beat matched, but after a few days of playing around, I was getting a lot better than those horrendous early attempts on my turntables.

Later that month, my friend DJ Josh Sparber came to visit, and he, too, inspired me to start DJing. When I told him I felt my mixing skills weren't there yet, he said the most important part of DJing was having good taste in music. Mixing techniques would follow suit, and as long as you had a great song selection, you were good to go. A few weeks later, I had dinner with DJ Lina Bradford, a major fixture on the island who also told me mixing would come later.

I reached out to the owner of Cherry's and asked her if I could DJ their Friday night disco party one night. The party had been going on forever, and even though they felt the bar was fine just using the mixtapes they'd been using since the '80s, she let me spin there one night. A bunch of friends came down for my set, and it went over well. I was hooked and decided I would start being more proactive about seeking out DJ gigs.

Today, one of my favorite parties to DJ is Below Tea — a classic disco party hosted by cable access pioneer Robin Byrd. I'm able to play the tracks I grew up listening to for a crowd of younger gays who aren't familiar with them, along with older gays who danced to them the first time around. The party attracts a lot of men in their fifties and sixties, and my heart fills with joy whenever I see an older couple doing the hustle.

In my time DJing on Fire Island, I've spun at every venue, including Cherry's, the Tiki Bar, the Island Breeze, the Ice Palace, Low Tea at the Blue Whale, Sip N Twirl and the Pavilion. One of the most interesting parties I ever DJed was Blow, a party that featured porn stars having sex on stage. Since the party took place on Fire Island — aka the land of no boundaries — there were some interesting moments to say the least.

Like the time a porn star came on stage carrying chicken fingers during what was supposed to be a sex scene. Baffled, the host had him squirt ketchup on his scene partner to dip the chicken fingers in before he ate them. Or the time a methed-out porn star freaked out and ran out of the club before he even went on. Or that time my sixty-five-year-old neighbor walked on stage and stuck his finger in one of the porn star's bungholes. Or my personal favorite: the time an angry patron took a shit in the back room to get revenge at the bar for throwing him out the week before.

It's times like this I realize DJing has connected me to my gay roots more than I ever could have imagined. Sometimes, when I'm DJing a disco set, watching the sun go down as China twirls about in a sequined dress, it makes me think of all the drag queens and mustachioed men who've danced on Fire Island ever since I was a little kid watching Dance Fever. And on those nights I decide to dress in drag, you can bet it's Darcel from *Solid Gold* I'm channeling as I whip my hair back and forth . . .

Playing disco as China and Zola enjoy the sunset at the Tiki Bar.
China was 121 years old in this pic.

EVERYTHANG!

I know I've been on Fire Island too long when I get back from a jog on the beach and scream, "That run was **EVERYTHANG**!"

GHPLEASE

Don't get me wrong. I love living on Fire Island all summer long. As any New Yorker will tell you, the city starts smelling like a homeless person's asshole somewhere around the Fourth of July, and only returns to its natural rotting garbage aroma sometime after Labor Day. So why would I choose to live in malodorous Brooklyn when I could be sniffing ocean breezes, writing this very essay one hundred yards from the ocean?

There *are* downsides to living in a resort town, though. It can sometimes get lonely, and occasionally I'll wake up with "Island-itus" and need to get the fuck off the island before I turn into Jack Torrance in *The Shining*. Also, businesses in resort towns attract a lot of workers who just want to party, and I often run out of things to talk about with them. There's only so many times I can have a conversation that starts with, "Gurl, Monet Exchange turnt it last night! All the children were gagging when she came out in that Sia wig, trust!"

Another problem with living on Fire Island is that every damn gay in the world goes there to party their face off. The island's always had a reputation for being a place where you can dance until the sun comes up and stumble home with a man or two every night of the week. Unfortunately, over the years, that allure has grown, and now, guys seem to think their weekend's a bust if they don't fuck fifteen guys and get medevac-ed off the island. Being a semi-adjusted forty-something, neither of these ideas appeal to me. Sure, I love to have a few drinks and entertain the occasional gentlemen caller, but I'm more about day drinking than staying up until 10 AM these days. Plus, as I mentioned earlier, I'm a weirdo gimp who gets sick unless I take ridiculous care of myself.

But since people on social media know I live on the island, I'm constantly being bombarded with texts, Facebook messages, Twitter and Instagram DMs and drop-by visits from people who only have forty-eight hours on the island and expect me to party with them . . . on a *Tuesday*.

There I'll be, having dinner, and I'll hear, "Greg! Are you home?! We were passing by and figured we'd drop by on our way to see Hedda Lettuce! Come with us!"

Bitch, I'm tryina work out at 8 AM before it's 90 degrees up on this piece tomorrow, so *no* I do *not* want to go to see Hedda's show for the twelfth time and do coke in the bathroom until 4 AM. It's a Tuesday! Besides, if I did this every time a friend swung by with this offer, I would be dead by the Fourth of July.

If it's a weekend, I might be more apt to indulge in some depravity. I have no problem indulging in a few too many drinks or dancing 'til 4 AM when the mood strikes me. But it's just not something I want to do every night of the week cuz it's no fun waking up feeling like roasted dog crap when it's 94 degrees and 92 percent humidity. Also, have I mentioned *I am 46 years old?* But age doesn't stop a lot of these gays from partying their Botoxed faces off. Sadly, I've lost track of how many guys I've seen OD at the bars and on the boardwalks. And sometimes, the ODs come straight to my house!

The most memorable time this happened was in 2013, when my friend Harry rented a house in The Pines with some friends of his from Los Angeles. Although he'd been coming to the island for years, Harry's friends had never been. He always held prestigious jobs, but loved coming to the island to . . . let off some steam, shall we say. Needless to say, his tawdry tales of hook-ups and drug binges had them primed. By the time they got to the island, they had two cases of vodka shipped to the house and brought $500 worth of coke, five vials of Special K, a bunch of molly and GHB.

Although I've tried just about every drug, GHB was never on my radar. From what I've heard, I have no interest in ever trying it, either. Due to a chemical reaction, if you ingest alcohol while you're on it, you can OD. As a semi-alcoholic, the idea of going to a bar and not being able to drink — or to *remember* not to drink when high on some drug — is not for me. That's why I've never tried it, even though lots of guys have told me, "It makes your body feel like you're on poppers and coming at the same time." Um? *Yes, please.*

Harry arrived with his friend Mike before the rest of the guys got to the island on a Friday morning. Later that day, they passed me by while I was reading on the beach. My jaw dropped when I saw this 6'2", 210-pound man with a perfectly chiseled, hairy chest heading towards my chair. As he got closer, I noticed Mike was wearing a speedo which perfectly outlined his bulging manroot. (Yes, I just used the word, *manroot*, which I've wanted to use ever since I saw it in a story in *Manshots* magazine in 1991.)

As I got to know Mike, I discovered he was a rarity — a drop-dead gorgeous man who was also completely down-to-earth. I invited them back to the house for a drink so Mike could meet Paul and Carl, who just got to the island. We had a nice time catching up while drinking Carl's signature drink — Vodka Soda Splasha Cran. Around six, Harry and Mike headed back to The Pines to pick up his friends. He wanted to get them to the house and bring them back to the harbor in time for tea.

For those of you not familiar with Fire Island and its traditions, low tea, middle tea and high tea are happy hours that take place in The Pines between 4 PM and 10 PM. Back in The Grove, things are a lot less structured, and you can have a drink any time of day. But in The Pines, low tea takes place between 4 PM and 8 PM at the Blue Whale, while high tea and fun tea take place between 7 PM and 10 PM at Sip N Twirl, and around the pool deck. If you happen to go to one location at a different hour, you might find it completely empty – or even worse — not even open. Coming from The Grove, this always seemed a little bizarre, but it's surely a Fire Island tradition.

A newer rite of passage is attending the Underwear Party at the Ice Palace on Friday nights. Harry planned to take Mike and his friends to the party after they hit tea and had the requisite 10 PM dinner of grilled chicken and vegetables. Paul and I had friends arriving the next morning, so we decided to skip the party so we could pick them up from the ferry without feeling totally busted. Besides, the party is insanely packed to begin with, and on holiday weekends it gets so crowded you can hardly move without getting dermabrasion from scraping against all the stubbly backs you have to wrestle your way through to get a drink. Instead, we had friends over for dinner and were in bed by midnight, looking forward to starting our Saturday without a hangover for once. By 1 AM, we were deep in REM sleep.

An hour later, I heard someone open the door to our bedroom.

"Greg? Paul? Are you awake?"

"Huh?" I asked.

"It's Harry. Mike is ODing on your deck."

Paul and I jumped out of bed.

"What?" Paul asked.

From outside, we heard Mike screaming: "FUCK ME! OH MY GOD FUUUUUUUUCK ME!"

Our heads turned in unison.

"What's going on?" Paul asked.

"Follow me," Harry said.

We rushed outside to find Mike screaming at the top of his lungs, cowering behind the tomato plants.

"OH MY GOD! FUCK ME! FUCK ME! I CAN'T TAKE IT ANYMORE!"

We soon learned Mike had accidentally taken a sip of his boyfriend's drink while on GHB at the Underwear Party. Harry thought he could get him back to The Pines before he fell out, but on the way there — around the time they were passing our house, actually — Mike started convulsing, screaming like a maniac and ODing. And now, he was standing there, right behind our heirloom tomato plants in his underwear, having a psychotic episode. Since I had no experience with people who OD on GHB, I had no idea what to do. Paul and I looked at one other, and then realized our living room was filled with Harry's friends, who were sitting on the couch as if nothing was going on.

We went into the living room and Harry introduced us.

"Hey guys. This is Gary, Angel, Richard and Kyle," he said as if we were in a perfectly normal situation. "Gary is Mike's boyfriend," he added.

"Um, hey?" I said.

"FUCK FUCK FUCK FUCK OH GOD!" Mike shouted from the deck.

"So what should we do?" I asked.

"Oh, he'll be fine. It just has to run out of his system," Gary said nonchalantly.

"What?" I barked. "I don't think that's a good idea. He is obviously ODing and I'm not having someone die in my house because you think he'll be fine!" I ran into my bedroom, got my iPhone and dialed 911.

While this was going on, Paul was outside on the deck trying to cajole Mike into coming out from behind the tomato plants.

"OH GOD, OH GOD! I'M GONNA DIE! FUCK ME! FUCK ME FUCK ME!" he shrieked at the top of his lungs.

Paul got his arms around Mike's sweat-drenched body and dragged him into the living room. When he placed him on the floor, Mike started to dry heave. Paul had to hold him up as his callous friends looked on as if they were watching an episode of *Murder She Wrote*.

I finally got through to 911 and gave them our address. Within minutes, we heard the fire alarm go off, signaling help was on the way. We placed a bucket in front of Mike as his body continued to convulse. Seconds felt like minutes felt like hours, and still no medical team! I seized on this moment to ask Gary why he was being so blasé.

"Oh, this happens all the time. In half an hour, he'll be fine. You really shouldn't have called the police. Do you have a place I can stash this coke?" he asked as he pulled out a vial of cocaine.

Instantly, his friends got up and unleashed bags of K and coke they were holding, hoping for hiding places, too.

When the medical team arrived with the police, they started tending to Mike as the police asked us questions.

"So what did he take?" they asked. The room fell silent. I was aghast. Knowing what he was on could help save his life, so I didn't hesitate.

"He was on GHB and mixed it with alcohol," I told them.

The medics nodded and one of them said, "Thanks. Now let's get him onto this stretcher and down the stairs."

Mike started muttering as the four of them tried to get him strapped onto the stretcher. Thankfully, his Tourette syndrome had now dissipated. The medics asked if anyone wanted to come with him, and his gross boyfriend actually hesitated before saying he would go. They took him to a nearby hospital after he was boated off the island, where he recovered and was given a bill for $6,000 the next morning. By 2 PM, he was back in The Pines.

You can imagine my surprise when I went to meet Harry for a drink at high tea that night and saw Mike drinking a vodka soda right next to him.

"The recovery from a G overdose is easy! Since you don't drink, you don't have a hangover," he said.

I was speechless. If I had put my gimp body through that, something tells me I would have taken me more than nine hours to bounce back . . . or show my face in public.

The shocks continued when Harry came up and said, "You know, Greg, all I could stare at last night when you and Paul were running around the apartment were the hard-ons poking through your underwear."

Once again, I was speechless.

The next day, Mike came over to ~~get his friends' drugs back~~ give us a bottle of vodka to thank us for taking care of him. But we told him it was us who should be thanking *him*. All weekend long, neighbors were congratulating us for having such a hot three-way.

"I don't know what you guys were doing to that guy, but it sounds like he was just *begging* for it!" they said.

"Well, I'm glad I could help boost your cache," Mike said.

"Us, too," Paul said. "And, most importantly, I'm glad you didn't ruin one of our heirloom tomatoes. You could have dropped dead, but if one of those got bruised, I would have been devastated."

MUUMUU LAND

Zing! The stinging text notification roused me from my slumber. Damn. What time was it? 3 AM? Ugh. Who was texting me at 3 AM? It was either one of my DJ friends, or my drag daughter, Tara Hole Jenkins, sending me some meme featuring a drag queen giving side eye.

When I reached for my phone, I saw it was indeed from Tara Hole Jenkins, aka Chad. "OMG! I got all these caftans for five dollars! I'm gonna bring them next week when I come visit you!" Along with the text was a video of Chad in said caftan prancing down Sixth Avenue in broad daylight.

This video was one of the reasons I loved having Chad in my life. The two of us instantly hit it off a few years ago when I hired him to be in a music video for one of my songs. Chad has a classically handsome, rugged look. He also looks like someone who might beat you up and rob you after a hookup. Classic rough trade.

Ironically, the first time I met him, he sashayed right into my apartment, opened his mouth, and his purse fell out. Turned out that *he* was a big *she*, and I loved the combination of masc/femme energy he exuded.

"Oh my God. This apartment is so cute! I love it! What a view! Oh my God! Is that a Kind bar? Can I have one? I'm *starving*," he said.

We became fast friends, and Paul and I started inviting him to holidays and dinner parties. Chad and I texted all the time —

sharing funny GIFS, spilling the tea, and helping each other when times got rough. Which is why I should haven't been shocked it was him texting me at three in the morning . . . again.

I snapped the phone to silent mode, threw it on my nightstand and fell back to sleep before I had a chance to read the other drunken texts which came in over the course of the next hour. When I woke up in the morning, I saw that I got four more texts from Chad, featuring three pictures of him wearing the caftans around the city, capped off with a meme of Ryan Gosling with the words "U Up?" sent at 4:32 AM.

I got on with my day and didn't think about the caftans until the following weekend, when Chad came to stay with us for the Fourth of July. Our friend Johnny was staying with us, too, since he was now addicted to doing the Invasion and flew in from LA every year to do it.

When Chad got to the house, he kept going on and on about the caftans, and I promised him we would have a "Caftan Dinner" once we were done with the Invasion. I knew most of our time would be spent styling wigs, helping Johnny put his topical lewk together and reteaching Paul how to walk in heels.

The day after the Invasion, Chad was all excited about our dinner. He brought out the caftans, and I must say, they really were colorful and pretty. Paul, Johnny, and Carl were less enthused — in fact, I'd venture to say they couldn't care less. I threw on the animal-print one Chad selected for Levonia and poured some wine as he pranced around the living room.

"Come on, guys! It'll be fun! Put one on!" I told Paul, Carl and Johnny, who were not feeling it.

"Um . . . maybe in a little while," Johnny said as he scrolled through Instagram.

"What? Put *that* on?" Carl asked, taking a break from reading us appalling Facebook updates.

"After I'm done cooking," Paul said — the only valid answer in my opinion.

Chad and I weren't bothered. We started prancing around the house with our wine like supermodels, reveling in the instant transformation slipping this cheap piece of fabric over our heads brought on. Our happiness was contagious. A few minutes later, I saw Johnny saunter over to the caftans to figure out which one might complement his summer tan. Five minutes later, he emerged from the bathroom with a big smile on his face.

"I kind of like this! This is fun!" he said as he did a twirl in the living room. That did it. Carl, the king of FOMO, was sold.

"I want one! The pink one!" he said as he darted over to the pile of caftans and put one on.

An hour later, we posed for this picture on our deck:

Chad, Carl, me, Paul and Johnny during the Caftan Dinner.
I love Chad trying to look all butch.

Putting on those cheap polyester caftans transformed our evening into something fun and playful. Johnny dubbed us "The Real Housewives of Cherry Grove" and it turned a cloudy, grey day into something joyful.

After we finished dinner, I suggested we hit tea in The Pines in our caftans. By this point, everyone was drunk and agreed. We cleaned the kitchen, made some to-go drinks and started trekking through the Meat Rack to get there. Years ago, the Meat Rack was filled with men cruising for sex, but thanks to hookup apps, it was now filled with more rabbits and foxes than bears and otters. We crossed the rack without seeing one fisting session.

When we landed in The Pines, we were met with nasty glances and comments.

"Oh, look, a bunch of bottoms!" someone screamed as his friends looked at us in horror. Ugh. Bottom shaming. Cue the internalized homophobia. Sadly, even in a gay paradise like Fire Island, you sometimes ran into people who had problems if you challenged their concept of gender norms. Anything that might not fit into their limited view that all gay men should be Masc 4 Masc can sometimes trigger an outburst.

When we finally landed on the dance floor at Sip N Twirl, we were met with equally unwelcoming looks from a lot of guys. I didn't care. I told everyone to join hands. We formed a circle and began twirling under the disco ball while bowing and raising our hands to the sky in adulation of whatever spirit had possessed us aka white wine. When we were done, we marched through the crowd holding hands and left within two minutes. There was no way I was hanging around a bunch of judgmental bores.

We made our way to the Pavilion, where DJ Vito Fun was spinning his eclectic party mix. Once again, we made our way to the center of the dance floor and started holding hands while spinning in a circle. The crowd was little less rude here — in fact, a few guys actually smiled. We kept dancing and after a few songs, went to get a drink. On our way to the bar, we got a few more evil glances from uptight men who were apparently offended by our very existence.

"Let's head back to The Grove. These people are a buzzkill," Chad said.

We agreed. I looked at my watch and realized a water taxi was literally one minute from arriving.

"Quick! Get to the dock! We could be home in like ten minutes!" I shouted. We all started running for the water taxi.

As we were exiting the club, a guy with a 'roided out body was prancing a few steps ahead of us, singing along to Whitney Houston's "How Will I Know?"

I said, "Excuse me, queen" as I tried to brush past him.

He grabbed me by the shoulders. "Who you calling a queen?!??
I'm not a queen!" he shouted in my face.

"Um . . . whatever, we're late for a boat," I said as Chad and I slithered past him and ran for the ferry. #'RoidRage mixed with #InternalizedHomophobia. Cute.

Thankfully, we made it to the water taxi and posed for an impromptu photo shoot as the boat zipped over the bay. The second we landed in The Grove, the reception to our caftans was noticeably improved.

"Yes, queens, work!" someone shouted as we exited the boat.

"Look! My Aunt Rosemary is here with all her friends from Ronkonkoma!" another person shouted.

We made our way over to Cherry's, which was in full swing. I led everyone through the crowd to the center of the dance floor to form our dance circle. This time, everyone started circling around us and joining in. Two lesbians leapt into the middle of the circle and started making out as we twirled around them. The fun was infectious and people started running up to us.

"I want to try one on! Can I wear it for a little while?" a stranger asked me.

"Oh my God! I love coming to The Grove! You never know what's gonna happen," a day-tripper told Chad.

We spent the rest of the night at Cherry's in our cheap five dollar lewks reveling in the joy a little bit of spontaneity could bring.

So I guess the moral of the story is: Pines queens suck donkey dong. JK LOL

Update: Our caftan dinner took place in 2015, and by the summer of 2018, gender norms had changed drastically. All summer long, I kept seeing guys in caftans and drag all over The Pines. Thanks, RuPaul. And Obama. And society. Oh, and *every queen who's been running around in drag in The Grove since like 1938*. Side eye emoji.

WHAT'S THE TEA?

Although I may sometimes come across like I'm disparaging The Pines, it's mainly in jest. To be honest, I'm just toying with stereotypes that have existed on the island for years. The truth is I have a major hard-on for a lot of the homes (and men) of The Pines. In fact, some days, instead of jogging the perimeter of The Grove like I usually do, I'll zigzag through The Pines so I can take in some of the beautiful houses along the way. Without fail, I always wind up stopping a few times when I come across a beauty I've never seen.

In the 1960s, an architect named Horace Gifford designed a lot of homes in The Pines, and I'm always thrilled when I get invited to a party in a space he worked on since they're each masterpieces of midcentury modern design. In fact, sometimes, I'll launch SCRUFF after my run, hoping I wind up hooking up with a guy in a Horace Gifford home. I'll even lower my standards if it's a house I haven't been in yet!

Another thing I love about The Pines is the infamous tea dances that take place at the Blue Whale, Sip N Twirl and the Pavilion, where I've been lucky enough to DJ over the years. The men who vacation in The Pines are usually fitness-conscious, and the stock of men who show up at tea can truly be stunning. A lot of men go to tea to cruise and pick up, and it's fun to see them meet and leave together as I watch from the DJ booth.

Although there have been tons of amazing DJs in Fire Island Pines over the years, DJ Lina is still considered the reigning queen.

Her tea dances are legendary, and filled with a positive, uplifting vibe that comes from her energy. Lina always makes sure to lock eyes with everyone who comes to her parties to let them know they're in a place where love and positive energy rule. She also puts a lot of effort into showing up in lewks that leave the children gagging.

I quickly clicked with Lina the second I met her. The two of us have strong personalities and a similar joie de vivre. For fun, I would head over to her parties and carry a drag outfit in my backpack. I'd say hello, dance as a guy for an hour, and then head into the bathroom where I'd throw on a wig, a bikini and a pair of sunglasses. Then I'd go back to the dance floor and put on an impromptu "performance" as Lina looked on, loving the homage.

I've had some of the best times of my life in Fire Island Pines, whether it be at Lina's tea dances, house parties, or dancing at the annual Pines Party all night long. And thanks to DJ Lina, who paved the way for an acceptance of all gender identities, drag and trans people are a lot more accepted in the Pines today. In fact, lately, whenever I show up in heels, I'm greeted by a lot of gays who are thrilled to see someone who's just there to have fun and queen out. And that's the tea, girl, *truss*.

SLIP N FALL

At the western end of Fire Island Boulevard in The Pines, the end of the boardwalk is capped off with a wooden bench that was installed fifteen years ago. Before that, the boardwalk just ended, leading to a green, algae-covered swamp. If you happened to be walking down the boards on a cloudy night, you had an 80-percent chance of landing in that swamp. Especially back in the '90s, when no one had flashlights on their phones like they do today.

Now, whenever I walk around Fire Island at night, I feel like I'm on the Long Island Expressway. Every five seconds, some moron is blinding me with the flashlight on their phone. Instead of pointing it *at the ground* to see where they're going, they hold it *directly in front of them* for some inane reason. But before everyone had a klieg light on their iPhone, you had to know where that boardwalk ended, or you could wind up covered in muck. And since a lot of my friends like to drink, I have firsthand knowledge of just how horrifying this can be.

The first time I experienced a friend of mine transforming into a Swamp Thing, I was having dinner in The Pines with Bring It and his friends, Tim and Michael. Bring It and Tim came out to visit Michael on a Wednesday night, and I was excited to see them. We had a great time catching up at Michael's house over cucumber margaritas and tacos. Bring It was his usual zany self, getting drunk and entertaining us with shows as he marched down the stairs lip-synching to Kylie Minogue. Tim, who I knew from years of doing coat check at NYC nightclubs, was his usual, affable self. He was sitting on the couch all night long, smoking, laughing, and occasionally chiming in with his signature line when he was at a loss for words, ". . . um . . . whatchamacallit?"

As in, "I was at the club the other night and I was talking to the . . . um . . . whatchamacallit?"

". . . the DJ?" Bring It replied, as Tim jumped in to agree.

"Right! The DJ and he was talking to the . . . um . . . whatchamacallit . . . the bouncer, right . . . " he'd go on, forgetting every eighth word and replacing it with whatchamacallit.

Since this was their first night in The Pines, Bring It and Michael decided they wanted to stay in instead of going into town so they could hit the beach without a hangover in the morning. I was fine with that, since I had to head back to the city the next day and didn't want to be a mess, too. Tim was not feeling it, though.

"You think I'm gonna sit around and stare at you three queens all night? I'm on Fire Island! I'm gonna go to . . . whatchamacallit. . . Sip N Twirl! I feel like dancing!" he announced.

"Fine, girl, have a blast dancing at Sip N Twirl at 11 PM on a *Wednesday*," Bring It replied. "We'll be here when you find out it's just you, the bartender and the *Now That's What I Call Dance! Volume 8* CD!" he taunted.

Not deterred, Tim headed into the night to get his groove on.

Ten minutes later, we heard him calling to us from the front door.

"Guys? Can you come here? I need your . . . um . . . whatchamacallit . . . your help."

Intrigued, the three of us went to see what was going on. Our faces dropped when we saw Tim standing there, covered in algae from head to toe.

"Queen!" Bring It screamed as he burst out laughing. "Did someone go for a *twirl* off the boardwalk after they had a few too many *sips*? Something tells me you did not pass Go, you did not collect two hundred dollars, but went straight to the Meat Rack to get some dick!"

We all cracked up.

"It's not funny!" Tim said. "But you're right," he added. "Now can one of you find a . . . whatchamacallit . . . a hose to spray me down? I don't want to get this crap all over the house. I'll never be invited back!"

Michael didn't waste a second. "Oh, I decided you weren't coming back when you showed up with that bottle of Smirnoff!"

"Very funny, bitch. You know you love the . . . whatchamacallit . . . the fun I bring!"

We laughed as Bring It started spraying Tim down. When he was algae-free, we headed to the hot tub so he could warm up as we polished off another round of cucumber margaritas.

Thankfully, the next summer, they installed that bench at the end of the boardwalk, which has saved countless queens from becoming . . . whatchamacallit . . . Swamp Things.

NOT MY FIRE ISLAND

In the spring of 2017, Logo released a trailer for their reality series, *Fire Island*. Within seconds, the gay internet reacted with an outrage only seen when Grindr and SCRUFF went down at the same time. A lot of the comments I read consisted of sentiments like, "Another minstrel show!" "Gays Gone Wild!" and my personal favorite, "NOT MY FIRE ISLAND!" It was as if the producers cast the show with Trump's cabinet instead of . . . camera-ready millennials?

In most cases, reality shows are cast with personalities who will either enrapture or enrage the audience. No one tunes into *Real Housewives of Atlanta* to see the ladies hold hands during a prayer circle. They watch because they want to see Kandi go awf when Marlo accuses her of being a lesbian during a glamping dinner party. It's the drama and drunken escapades that make reality shows work. And in this case, serve.

But the very same people who watch all the *Real Housewives* franchises were the same ones upset the *Fire Island* trailer featured over-the top personalities in salacious scenes. It was almost as if they expected *Fire Island* to be a Ken Burns documentary instead of a reality show featuring boys in speedos getting drunk at low tea and coming for one other during their gluten-free dinners.

A lot of people were also bothered because the show was cast with flamboyant twenty-somethings. As someone who works in television, I can attest the show would have been a lot less lively if it was filled with six scholars debating over whether we're living in a computer simulation or not. Sadly, a lot of comments I saw were also femme-shaming. Besides being concerned about their internalized homophobia, the men who posted things like "These guys are too gay" need to realize the LGBTQ community is represented by a rainbow — not one color. And while there were a lot of characters in that trailer, there were some who represented different shades.

People were also concerned the show would turn the island into a trashy tourist town à la Jersey Shore. First off, there's no way a fringe show like *Fire Island* would have the cultural impact of *Jersey Shore*. Secondly, last time I checked, Fire Island is already a trashy tourist town. If you don't believe me, come to the Ice Palace one holiday weekend when they run out of Fireball by noon. Lastly, a lot of these negative comments came from people who felt the show was "not their Fire Island."

As someone who has lived on the island all season long for many years, I agree the 1:15 trailer did not completely encapsulate my experience, but it did seem like a pretty good representation of what goes on. A lot of people come to party, while others visit to relax and unwind. And while I would rather watch a documentary about those artists who sketch nude dudes in the meat rack, pop culture spawned *Fire Island*, and I'm happy some TV executives chose to green-light a show featuring members of the LGBTQ community frolicking in their natural habitat instead of *Dating Naked: Toronto*.

RINSE AND REPEAT

A major draw of the Underwear Party at The Ice Palace in Cherry Grove is the notorious back room, as my sick and sadistic friend Matt discovered during his first visit. The end of the dance floor gets sectioned off with a scrim, and becomes a hotbed of sexual activity where lustful men can satisfy their carnal needs while listening to Ariana Grande. When the party begins, not a soul can be found there, but as the night goes on, people start getting the liquid courage they need to have anonymous sex. At midnight, everyone's on the dance floor drinking and carrying on. But come 2 AM, the dance floor is emptier than a Detroit factory because everyone's in the back room with their underwear around their ankles.

I'm not a fan of back rooms because I've never been one for anonymous sex. I get nervous in public, and usually come faster than a fifteen-year-old getting his first hand job behind a bowling alley. Also, I like to vet my sexual partners in a well-lit environment. It's dark back there and for all I know, I could be hooking up with someone with a herpes sore. Or Richard Simmons. Another reason I avoid the back room like carbs is because a lot of people on Fire Island know me, and the last thing I need is for someone to walk by with my dick in someone's mouth. But thanks to pickleback shots, that's just what happened to me in the summer of 2011.

That season was the year those delicious, briny shots first started showing up on the island, and for some reason I was completely unfamiliar with them. I usually drink vodka on nights I'm in for the long haul, and only have whiskey and scotch in the winter. But when the bartender coupled whiskey with that tasty pickle juice, I just about lost my mind. Carl and I must have downed six of them in the course of two hours. Fine for a German man with a constitution like his, but for a gimp like myself, not so much. I was full-on wasted by midnight.

When I realized how drunk I was, I dragged Carl onto the dance floor to try and sober up. We were dancing to Lady Gaga's "Poker Face" when I spotted a handsome guy checking me out from across the floor. We locked eyes, I made my way over and we started dancing.

"Hey, I'm Tony!" he shouted over the music.

"I'm Greg!" I drunkenly slurred back.

Tony was visiting from Philly. We exchanged a few more pleasantries and started making out. We soon realized we were pitching tents in our underwear and he suggested we go to the back room to take care of our burgeoning boners. I followed him behind the scrim, and before I knew it, he was on his knees going down on me in the middle of a sea of men. Everyone was either hooking up or cruising one another. Quickly, all of my back room fears started becoming realities: trolls started groping me, random weirdos kept trying to make out with me, and worst of all, people I knew were forming a circle around us.

One of the men who came by was Mark, a tall German man with a mop of blond I knew from the beach. I had zero interest in having sex with him because the last thing I want to do is hook up with someone I see every day. But apparently Mark didn't have the same reservations as I did, because he whipped his monstrous dick out and started playing with it right next to me. Tony saw the gorgeous ten-inch cock being stroked just inches from his face and quickly switched from going down on me to sucking off Mark. After he choked on Mark's length for the fifth time, Tony started giving me some attention, and then started taking turns blowing the two of us.

"Oh, great," I thought. "All I need is for someone I know to see this."

I was praying the whole thing would end, and thankfully it did. Before I knew it, Mark pulled his dick out of Tony's mouth and started jacking off. A few strokes later, he started shooting ropes of cum all over Tony's face. He kept *coming* and *coming*, and before I knew it, he had covered Tony's *entire face and head* with jizz.

Tony's face went from a state of ecstasy to one of grave concern as he got coated with one last glob. He opened his eyes and tried to figure out how much cum he had on his head. When he realized he was coated like a vanilla frosted cake, I caught him looking around, trying to figure out what to do. He didn't have a shirt or a rag to clean himself off with; all he had was his underwear. He wiped some of it off with his hand as he realized he had to go through the club with a head covered in spooge to reach the bathroom and wash off.

I pulled my underwear up and grabbed him by the hand. I told him to act like he was about to throw up, and we made our way to the bathroom so we could clean his face off in one of the stalls. But that hair. It made the scene in *There's Something About Mary* seem tame. While we were figuring out what to do, I remembered the pool at the Ice Palace opened at 2 AM during the Underwear Party. We darted out of the stall, ran to the pool and jumped in. Before we knew it, Tony was back to normal. We dried off, headed to the bar and shared a laugh while having one last pickleback shot. As I swigged the tasty shot down, I made a note to myself: don't ever go into a back room without a bandana.

TABLE FOR TWO

In the past few years, the advent of PrEP has greatly changed the landscape of gay sex. Now that people are armed with a tool that greatly reduces their chances of contracting HIV, the fear that's surrounded sex for a lot of gay men since the '80s has started to fade away. That, coupled with the fact that HIV meds have made positive men undetectable and unable to pass the virus, has made it a lot more enjoyable for gay men to partake in casual sex again.

This became rather apparent in the summer of 2016, when I realized every friend of mine was having sex with a different person every day of the week. It also seemed like every bar and club had a weekly party that centered around sex, and people were blowing each other every time I went to the bathroom when these parties weren't even going on.

Don't get me wrong. Sex has always been a major part of Fire Island. In fact, for some men, it's the only reason they come. And although the Underwear Party has always had a back room, I recently started feeling as though I was transported back to the year 1978, when sex was all over the island. The summer of 2016 was the first year it seemed there were more people in the back room than on the dance floor at the Underwear Party, and sex could be had just about anywhere inside or outside the bar.

This couldn't have been any clearer than the night I was talking to my friend Taylor on the outdoor deck of the Ice Palace during the Underwear Party. The two of us were having a heated discussion about *RuPaul's Drag Race* — as gays do —when I realized a man's head had inserted itself into our conversation. The head was about a foot and a half below mine, and since I had a few drinks, it took a moment to realize it was staring directly into my face while I was talking to Taylor. Before I could try and figure out what was going on, the head started bobbing back and forth with a dazed look in its eyes.

"Oh my God, I think that guy next to you is getting fucked," I told Taylor, who took a drag off his cigarette and inadvertently elbowed the guy in the face.

"Oh, sorry," he said as we turned to see what was going on. Taylor stepped back to reveal a man directly behind this dazed, floating face, fucking him like there was no tomorrow. The top winked and smiled at us as I looked down and realized the guy getting fucked had no idea what was going on because he was so high.

"This is totally bizarre," I told Taylor as we took a few steps back to give them some space. "This is the first time someone actually tried to fuck himself into a conversation I was having!"

"Girl, I don't think that one is interested in having a conversation right now," Taylor said as we moved away from the show that was now attracting an audience.

Now, I completely understand if you want to have sex in the back room of an underwear party, but to do it in the middle of an open area where people are trying to talk about Detox getting sent home after lip-synching for her life on *RuPaul's Drag Race All Stars* and listening to Madonna's "Vogue" is a little much, no? I mean, read the room! If you're looking to get your hole plowed out, there's a space designated for that *fifteen feet away*! And if you're lucky, the DJ will segue into Ariana Grande's "Into You" by the time your G'd-out ass staggers over there.

Later that night, Taylor and I went to an underground party being held in the Meat Rack. As we made our way toward the party, we heard the distant thump of house music from the center of the forest. We entered a clearing and saw that trees had been lined with lanterns and a makeshift dance floor had been created with a string of rope lights in the sand. About seventy-five guys were partying in the woods under the stars. I looked up and saw a crescent moon on the horizon and realized I was having one of those special nights one can only have on Fire Island. As I looked back down into the crowd, I realized eight guys were daisy-chain fucking in the center of the dance floor.

Watching them jerk and heave like wild animals didn't make me think of a mind-blowing porno, but for some reason, *The Human Centipede*. Once again, I felt like I was transported to the year 1978, when men were having sex all over the island. But this time, thanks to Truvada, HIV meds and the occasional condom, everyone was going to be just fine.

BUKKAKE BOY

Sunday afternoons are bittersweet for a lot of weekend warriors. Friday and Saturday come and go quickly, and for some, it's time to head back to the city on the 4:45 PM ferry before they know it. I always like to walk Paul down to the ferry landing to see him off on Sunday afternoons before he heads back home to Brooklyn. A lot of other people go back on that boat, and I usually wind up saying goodbye to lots of friends while I'm there. It's about an hour and a half's journey back to the city, and most people like to get home early on Sunday so they can start their work week refreshed.

One Sunday, while we were waiting for the ferry, our neighbor John ran up to us, completely out of breath.

"Oh, thank *God*," he said. "I thought I was going to miss it!"

He wiped the sweat from his brow and I realized he had something else on his forehead: a gob of cum.

"Um, John, you might want to wipe a little further back," I said.

He giggled. "Ooh, bukkake boy just had some fun in the Meat Rack! I guess I missed a spot! I spent the afternoon in the woods, and before I knew it, it was 4:30 and I had to run to catch the ferry! I have a business dinner tonight I can't miss." He wiped his brow again. "Is it all gone?" he asked.

I assured him he was fine and everyone boarded the ferry.

As the boat pulled away, I got a text from Paul. "Bukkake *boy*? That man is easily 60." I texted him back. "God bless. If I'm sucking dick in the Meat Rack at 60, I'd be running around with that pearly badge of honor, too."

GOLDEN TIME OF DAY

In the summer of 2017, there was an artist on the island collecting urine from men on the beach so he could distill their piss into a certain color of yellow oil paint from the 1500s or some shit. Fine. Then I found out a leather daddy on the island decided to throw him a party so he wouldn't get in trouble for having guys pee in his bucket on the beach. Still all good. But then I found out that the leather daddy decided to sing *opera* in a *harness* at
the pee party and that's when my head exploded.

.

OH, DEER!

One morning, I walked into my garden with a cup of tea and saw my precious cat, Venus watching a deer eating shrubs in our garden. Venus tentatively walked over to the edge of the boardwalk, edging closer to the fawn. Slowly, but surely, the deer came up to her and they shared a cute little kiss.

. . . What? I can't have one fucking story that doesn't end with someone ODing on my roof while dressed as Liza Minelli?!?!?

Venus getting ready to give a tick-riddled deer a kiss.

COMMUNITY

Although I'm a rather social person, I don't participate in a lot of community activities. Now before you think I'm some kind of monster, let me explain. I've always been more of a city person, and the small-town mentality a lot of people on Fire Island have turns me off. People can be petty, and a lot of gays love to start drama over things that don't really matter. Bitch, I will GO AWF if someone tries to rope me into that mess, so I like to keep my distance. Instead, I like to donate money to fundraisers and donate items for auctions.

That said, I love so many people in the Cherry Grove community. Most of them work hard for important issues like breast cancer, prostate cancer and the Dunes Fund, which raises money to help buffer the town from storm damage. And when the town is faced with tragedies, like the AIDS crisis, Hurricane Sandy, or the mass shooting at Pulse nightclub, that's when it is amazing to live in a community filled with people who love and support one another when things look bleak.

One of my fondest memories on Fire Island was the weekend after the shooting at Pulse. The leaders of the community decided to hold a candlelit vigil, and hundreds of people came down to the ferry landing to pay their respects to the fallen. Watching a sea of candles light up the night in silence, as we gathered with our brothers and sisters to start the healing process, will stay with me the rest of my life.

More importantly, it was the one time I was able to put my arm around that bitch Valerie while that asshole Bobby wasn't running his Goddamned mouth about how Gary gave him the side-eye at the prostate cancer luncheon because he didn't vote for him for to be Homecoming Queen.

Candlelit Vigil on the dock in Cherry Grove, 2016.

PETTYCOAT JUNCTION

Over the winter, I live my gay life in Brooklyn while daydreaming of moving back to Fire Island at the end of May. In that time, I don't give as much thought to the island as a lot of other people I know because I had to turn notifications off for the Facebook group I belong to: Cherry Grove Untucked. Although you would think it would be a great way to stay connected with the community during the off-season, I quickly realized most of the posts were from the same five trolls who just want to stir the pot.

Besides, during the summer, I get my full share of drama from Carl, who loves reading us scandalous updates from the group as his *cawfee* kicks in on Saturday mornings.

"Did you see the tea on Cherry Grove Untucked?" he'll ask. "Wait until you hear *this*! You're not gonna *believe it*!" Then he'll start telling us some appalling story he discovered.

Carl keeps me in the loop all summer long, and I know I'll find out all the major dirt that takes place over the winter during my first ferry ride back to The Grove over Memorial Day Weekend.

"Did you hear? Jack and Brian broke up! I never really saw them together."

"The Crab Shack tried to put an addition on their dining room, but they didn't have a permit and Brookhaven shut them down!"

"Jackie O'Crabsis must have given up smoking because girl, she put on fifty pounds!"

"Miss Conception moved her show to The Island Breeze. Guess she had enough of management mistreating her at Sunsets."

"Gary is drinking again."

And on and on.

My favorite scandal of the past few years involved someone's unhappiness with the recipients of the Cherry Grove Honorees Awards, which celebrates people who serve the community. Apparently, someone believed the people selected were not worthy of being revered for some bizarre reason.

This sad person then took it upon himself to make a flyer with their names on it followed by the words, *Who? What?* and *Why?* Oh, the shade! Then he put the flyers up around town on bulletin boards. Can you imagine? A grown man putting that much energy into tearing people down by printing flyers on his 1994 bubble jet home printer.

Adding fuel to the fire, Logan Hardcore, one of the drag queens on the island, took a picture of the flyer and posted it in Cherry Grove Untucked, fueling a full-on war between people who found the flyer abhorrent, and bizarre randos who applauded this person for "calling out hypocrisy in the community" which made no fucking sense.

Now although I said I like to stay out of petty drama, when Carl texted me about this shizz, you can best believe I read all *127* comments under the post, while sending Paul screen shots of the most vicious ones.

#THIRSTY

Since Cherry Grove and The Pines are small communities, it's easy to get wrapped up in the scene. If you have any semblance of social skills, you can meet just about everyone who parties on the island in two weeks and carve out your own niche in no time.

If you happen to care. I, personally, couldn't care less.

Although I'm a social person and "put myself out there" as my Uncle Mario likes to say, I don't need to be loved by everybody and have no interest in hanging out with people I have nothing in common with. I also happen to be someone who can't hide how they feel about people. If I find you repellent, you'll know. But others revel in the attention a small place like Fire Island can give them and have no problem forming loose connections with people they do not necessarily like or get along with.

Unfortunately, a few years ago, I made the mistake of sharing a house with someone I barely knew. A mutual friend who was going in on the house assured me the two of us would get along famously, and after our initial meeting, it seemed that Drew and I were going to be fast friends. He was wildly handsome, charismatic, and liked to have a good time.

Four weeks later, I discovered Drew was also a complete and total social climber with no integrity. I'd cook meals for him and he'd *sleep through dinner*, get up at 11 PM and say it was too late to eat — then ignore me at the bar when he was hanging out with "the cool crowd" (LMFAO that he even *thought* there was a "cool crowd" in Cherry Grove) and basically wound up being a total douchebag. I'd see Drew at Cherry's, and he'd pretend not to know me as he did shots with some drag queen and her entourage.

Since I don't suffer fools, as soon as I got his number, he was dead to me. Sadly, it took everyone else the whole summer to figure him out. By that time, Drew had worked his way into every social circle and had broken a few hearts along the way. Then, after making all these people think he was their new best friend, he suddenly left when he found a boyfriend who only liked to vacation in South Hampton and never returned. (Praise be!)

Thankfully, after everyone discovered what a piece of shit Drew was, they started telling me all the dirt they had on him. You know what they say: If you don't have anything nice to say, *sit next to me.*

Of all the tawdry tales, my favorite was when someone told me Drew was so desperate for approval he let a bearded hipster pee down his throat in the bathroom of the Ice Palace. When I found out, I was saddened for this pathetic middle-aged man, yet also filled with joy like a five-year-old opening presents on Christmas morning. Hey, it's not my fault he was #ThirstierThanTheSaharaDesert.

WHEN BOTTOMS COLLIDE

As just about every homosensual in the civilized world knows, all you need to do is launch Grindr or SCRUFF any hour of the day if you wanna get laid. This is especially true on Fire Island, where just about every guy is on the Salem Dick Hunt from the second they board the ferry. Hookups are plentiful, and if you lower your standards, can be had with just three swipes on your iPhone. A conversation that goes something along the lines of:

"Looking?"

"Yeah."

"Host?"

"Yeah."

"Address?"

"789 Ocean" is usually all it takes.

Call me crazy, but I like to trade a few messages with a potential hookup to try and make sure this person is not a serial killer. But for other guys, the only thing that matters is that the person he's chatting with has a working dick or hole.

Carl can sometimes fall into the latter category. We'll stumble home from the bars at 4 AM, and while we're devouring leftover pasta directly from of the fridge, he'll tell me he just set up a hookup in the fifty-five seconds since we've been home. Or I'll have to grab him as he almost falls off the boardwalk while checking Grindr messages at 3 AM to see if anyone contacted him since he previously checked the app five minutes ago. I'm always secretly thrilled when he has these poorly-vetted, late-night trysts because it usually means I'll get a story the next morning.

Some of his failed hookups can be summed up in a singles sentence, like: "I fell asleep with Grindr on," "I got to the house and he was coked out," "He was thirty pounds heavier than his pictures," "I walked through his screen door and he threw me out," and my personal fave, "I didn't realize he was on Long Island."

In my experience, exchanging a few messages on a hookup app is usually all it takes to make sure I will be engaging in a satisfying sexual experience. It allows me to figure out a few pertinent details, like, for instance, if he's top or a bottom. Call me crazy, but that's just something I would figure out before heading to meet a stranger.

One of my favorite stories from Carl's vast catalog of Grindr hookups took place on a Saturday afternoon. While Paul and I were getting ready to go to the beach, Carl told us he was heading to The Pines to, quote, "see a friend" which we both knew was code for "have a hookup." Carl never went to The Pines, except for July Fourth, when a boat would haul him and three hundred other men dressed in drag there for the Invasion. He would stay in The Pines so he could drink for free, and then stumble home through the Meat Rack a few hours later.

So you can imagine our surprise when Carl found us on the beach just twenty minutes later.

"Well that was quick," I said as he plopped himself down on the blanket.

"You're never gonna believe *this one*," he said. "So I get to his house, and we're making small talk, and he says, 'So I don't think this is going to work. Do you know why?' So I said, 'Yeah. Cuz we're both bottoms.' And he freaked out! 'Who the fuck do you think you are, calling *me* a bottom?!' he screamed. 'Well you are,' I told him. 'A bottom.'"

"You better get the fuck out of my house right now before I really lose it," the guy screamed back at him.

"Calm down, I'm leaving now . . . you *bottom!*" Carl taunted as he rose to leave.

His failed hookup turned red. "I can't believe you are calling me a —"

"Bottom? Cuz you are!" Carl said as he made his way through the living room and out of the house. "It's not a big deal! You're just a bottom! Admit it!"

"Fuck you! I hope I never see your face again!" the guy screamed.

"Me, too . . . *bottom!*" Carl shouted as he started walking to the boardwalk.

"Fuck you!" the guy screamed.

"I would fuck you, but you're a bottom!" Carl screamed, easily now five yards from his house.

"And I kept screaming 'bottom' at him, *cuz he was!*" Carl told us. "I'm not sure if he was in denial or just mad that I called him out on it, but there was no way in hell *she* was a *top!*" he said as he re-launched Grindr to try to find a more appropriate stranger to anally penetrate him.

TICK, TICK, BANG!

One of the most ironic things about Fire Island is that even though there are hundreds of men trying to hook up at any given moment, most of them can't host because they're sharing a house with thirty-three guys. That's why it's wise to find out if that uncut Latin top you're chatting with can have you over before you wind up with a case of blue balls.

For a few adventurous types, hooking up in the Meat Rack is always an option. As someone who's not a fan of public sex — especially in a place where I know a lot of people — the Meat Rack has never been for me. Besides, it's hot and sweaty in those woods, and you have to cover yourself with bug spray to keep the mosquitos and ticks away. Not. Sexy. At. All.

But for some, outdoor sex is a huge turn-on. Of course, despite my feelings on the matter, I recently found myself in the Meat Rack with my shorts around my ankles, having sex with a guy I met on SCRUFF.

It was a scorching August afternoon and I had friends in town. The house was full and there were people lounging on the outside deck and in the living room. We had just finished lunch and everyone was about to fall into a rosé-induced coma.

"I'm just gonna go into the bedroom to relax in the air conditioning for a little while," I told everyone after I finished doing the dishes.

In reality, I was sneaking off to launch SCRUFF cuz I was hoping I could find a guy I was interested in having sex with who could host. Those two requirements put my likelihood of this happening around three percent right off the bat. Normally, I would have a guy over to my place, but with a house full of people, it would be weird. Plus, I didn't need anyone witnessing that awkward, initial hookup small talk that always takes place before the dicks get whipped out.

Thankfully, Michael, a handsome guy I'd messaged with earlier in the week, was online. I hit him up and found out that he, too was looking to meet. Of course, it soon came to light he had six guys in his house and was sharing a bedroom with a friend who was currently taking a nap next to him, so he couldn't host either.

"AAAARGH!" I screamed inside. When I told Michael I also couldn't host, he suggested we meet up in the Meat Rack.

"I never did that before and I think it would be hot to blow our loads in the sand," he messaged.

Normally, this idea would be almost as repellent as the bug spray I would have to cover myself in so I didn't come back with Lyme disease, but since I was horny AF, I agreed, and like a moron, headed out in the 90 degree, 90 percent humidity to meet Michael.

"Be right back I have to get a USB I lent to a DJ friend who's in the Pines," I blurted to my friends as I darted out of the living room before anyone could question me any further on my pretty damn good lie. Normally, I wouldn't care if my friends knew I was going to hook up, but one of the people visiting was a straight girl from work and I didn't want to get into a whole discussion about what it's like to be in an open relationship with her just then.

Michael and I met by the bench outside the Meat Rack and found a place to play in the forest, far removed from the peering eyes of anyone who might be on the Salem Dick Hunt. He had a great dick, and it was kinda hot going down on him in the middle of the woods. We took turns blowing each other, and before I knew it, I was ready to explode. He jacked me off and when I came on his chest, he shot his load right between my knees in the sand. By the time I finished shooting, he was covered in sweat and cum. I wiped my jizz off his chest with the bandana I always carry around because I sweat like a maniac, and we went our separate ways.

Later that afternoon, as I was lying on the beach with Carl and my friends, my phone started blowing up with SCRUFF notifications.

"Oh no, my profile must have gotten thrown into the Global Grid!" I thought.

But instead, I picked up my phone and saw eight messages from Michael. Apparently, when he got back to the house, he found a tick on his shoulder and was freaking out. He told me I should look to see if any of them were on me. I got totally creeped out and made Carl check me over. Thankfully, he didn't find any, but I made him keep looking. As he was looking me out for the third time, I got more messages from Michael.

"Check yourself again. I found another one. Though I think the first one I found might not have been a tick. It was a fleck of dirt."

"This one was crawling up my neck."

"Now I feel like my skin is crawling."

The messages went on and on. "We were going to do mushrooms today, but now I'm all freaked out and can't think of doing them. This was such a terrible idea," he continued.

Gurl, I thought. Chill.

"Jesus," I said to Carl "the next time I decide to get dick in the Meat Rack, just tell me to jerk off! I mean, I'm not afraid of ticks. They've got nothing on this guy! This guy is latching on *tight!*"

For the next two hours, Michael kept torturing me with paranoid messages. Part of me felt bad for him, but part of me was like, "Why are you dragging me down your weird shame spiral, dude?" But since I'm a nice person, I continued replying to his messages to try and calm him down.

In a horrendous twist of fate, it turned out Michael lived ten blocks from me in Brooklyn. He found me on SCRUFF one afternoon when I was back in the city, and we started messaging. When I asked him if he wanted to meet up, he informed me he was waiting to get the results of a syphilis test because he found a rash. This guy had nothing on Debbie Downer.

Later in the week, I sent him a message to see how he was doing, and he told me the rash wound up being an allergic reaction to a new medicine and that all his tests came back negative. Then he started getting all weird, texting me about all the times he had STIs in the past. I humored him and kept messaging him back until he was done venting, and then told him I had to go. The next morning, I blocked him.

> ## Could we find like a bathroom around there you could fuck me in?

A desperate message I got from someone who couldn't host.

THE MORE YOU BLOW

I don't really have a story for this. I just thought it would make a good title.

BANG THAT BOX

Fire Island is riddled with wildlife. On any trip, you are just about guaranteed to see a deer, a fox, an eagle, an otter, a bear, or my favorite flight of fancy: legendary cable-access pioneer, Robin Byrd, known for her Leased Access television show, *The Robin Byrd Show*.

Whether you're on the beach, at tea, or shopping for groceries, you can usually spot Robin walking around with her dog, greeting everyone she passes with a smile, wearing a loose sarong or nothing at all.

As fate would have it, Robin and I started working together a few years ago at high tea in The Pines. Robin hosted as I spun, and the second we met, we clicked. I soon learned one of the reasons we got along so well is because we're both Aries flakes who love talking about how the moon is affecting our energy levels and how Mercury in retrograde screwed up our texts. We're very similar and both embrace life with an open heart and probably a little too much naivete.

One of my favorite memories of working with Robin that first summer was the night the two of us walked back to The Grove through the Meat Rack after work. As we marched through the Rack, Robin started blowing the whistle she used at tea, screaming, "Get your pants up! This is a raid, queens!" while the two of us laughed like two-year-olds.

Since then, I've shared countless moments that end with Robin and I laughing until our stomachs hurt, and I'm grateful she's been a fixture on Fire Island since her time on cable access in the '80s. She's a constant reminder that although Fire Island can be about sex, it's also about fun, which is just as important.

Robin hosting high tea in The Pines.

THANKS?

The summer after my first book was published, I asked FIG, a store in downtown Cherry Grove, if they would be interested in carrying it. They agreed, and the next weekend, I was thrilled to see my book displayed in their front window. About a month later, I was walking home from the beach when I ran into my neighbor, Austin.

"Oh my God! Am I glad I ran into you!" he said. "I got your book and I want you to sign it for me!" he went on.

"Cool!" I said. "Thanks! Did you get it at FIG?" I asked.

"No! Someone left it on the boardwalk. You know, where people put things out by the garbage?" he continued, not even remotely aware of how doubly insulting this was.

"Oh, " I said. "Great." Then I followed him into his house and signed his garbage-picked book.

GAMES PEOPLE PLAY

In order to amuse ourselves on Fire Island, my friends and I like to play games we come up with. Since so many characters frequent The Grove, we usually like to incorporate these unassuming people into our games. For instance, when lounging on the beach, we usually wind up playing a few rounds of these gems:

Where Did She Get That Mesh Bathing Suit?

Call Boy or Really Bizarre May/December Romance?

Is That Bulge a *Banana*?!?

And when we're at the bars, we always wind up playing:

How Many Days Has That Crystal Queen Been Awake?

How Did That Lesbian Describe That Haircut To Her Barber?

Is That Drag Queen's Wig From CVS or Duane Reade?

Is That Person With The Mullet From Long Island or Staten Island?

'Roids or Androgel?

. . . and my personal favorite, the simply titled, Toupee?

I know. We're evil. But you know you wanna play, too.

UPDATES

Since I first joined Facebook in 2008, I've posted about Fire Island a lot. Here's a random sampling of some updates I've shared:

Cherry Grove: Where International Male Exclusives come to play!

Just got to Cherry Grove. I haven't seen this many bad tattoos since Bombshell McGee's Tupperware party.

It's getting harder to detect the gender of some of the people in Cherry Grove so I just shout "Hey, Gurl!" and hope for the best.

You know you're on Fire Island when there's bath salt-encrusted salmon on the menu.

If the government needs torture tactics, they should just ask me to send over some of the houseguests I've had on Fire Island.

I love how this article only talks about how Grindr is hurting the bars in the Pines - they don't mention Cherry Grove because everyone here is an alcoholic.

Passed Wanda Sykes & Neil Sedaka during my morning run. Cherry Grove has arrived . . . in the years 2002 and 1974, respectively.

I love the look of shock & disgust I get when I tell guys from the Pines my house is in Cherry Grove.

The difference between working out with guys in The Pines vs The Grove is that I feel like Cristiano Ronaldo in the Grove and Gollum in the Pines.

Apparently the acceptable way to say goodbye to someone when you talk to them at a bar for thirty seconds on Fire Island is an open-mouthed kiss on the lips.

If someone comes back from Fire Island and says they had "a very relaxing time" it just means they snorted three bags of K.

Cherry Grove: Where people say "Good morning" at 3 PM.

Cherry Grove: Where people work the boardwalk like a runway when it's pitch black.

Nom nom nom. Living on Fire Island is getting to me: I just made an egg white omelet with Truvada sauce. It took no PrEP at all!

Down in Fort Lauderdale, where I keep thinking I see people I know from Fire Island who just turn out to be tan alcoholics.

I can tell fall has arrived on Fire Island because the nudists have miniature scarves around their dicks.

Back on Fire Island, where the men are on leashes and the dogs run free.

A lot of guys on Fire Island have gay face, but I just saw some queen who was serving up Gayest Face.

Only on Fire Island do you hear not one, but two gay men honestly try to use the excuse, "I had a heart attack" for not coming to your show.

So far, it appears the only damage Hurricane Irene has inflicted on the residents of Fire Island has been liver damage.

90% of the people on Fire Island would make great Shakespearian actors, given their propensity for monologues.

Overheard a great line last night at tea: "God, can't I have my public sex in private?!?"

Back on Fire Island and yup . . . nothing's changed . . . since 1979.

You know you're on Fire Island when you see a 60 year-old man wearing a Gossip Girl cut off T-shirt.

Him: "What do you do on Fire Island?" Me: "Make ice, do the dishes and pray the guests will leave."

First day back at SNL after 3 months on Fire Island. I know this because, so far, not one person has greeted me by waving their hand in my face while saying, "Girl. Not yet. I ain't had my coffee."

GARDEN SHED OF EARTHLY DELIGHTS

Many people think Fire Island is a magical place. Lifelong connections are made on a dance floor, synchronicities happen when you least expect them, and days and nights take wonderful turns that lead you to surprising places. The fact that these things happen in such a natural, beautiful setting makes these events seem even more enchanted. Whether it's dancing 'til dawn with a handsome stranger, watching a jaw-dropping lightning storm roll over Long Island, or stumbling upon long-lost friends on a trip to the Sunken Forest, magic is everywhere. But sometimes, the magic that's conjured is black.

On Sundays, I usually find myself alone after Paul and Carl leave on the 4:45 PM ferry. In years past, I would see them off, cook an early dinner and walk to the Pines for DJ Lina's disco classics night, Throw Black Sundays. I had no problem going by myself since I knew I would run into a few friends or meet some new ones when I got there. I also knew I would sweat out most of the booze I drank over the weekend by the time Lina wrapped up the party with Diana Ross's "The Boss."

One Sunday night, I made myself a to-go drink and headed through the Meat Rack as the sun started going down. I always loved walking through the forest that time of night, since nature — just like the gays — likes to put on shows, too. That night, the sun was turning both the clouds and the ocean orange. The entire forest was auburn, and I bounced along, listening to the ice clinking in my cup and taking it all in.

When I got to The Pines, I sat on the bench at the end of Fire Island Boulevard to bang the sand out of my sneakers and polish off the rest of my to-go drink. As I made my way down the road, I spotted a deer clomping down the sandy path that ran next to the boardwalk with a baby doe beside her. I could tell it was going to be a special night.

A few yards down the boardwalk, I saw a shirtless man standing at the intersection of Tuna Walk and Fire Island Boulevard. I always say hello to people when I pass them, something that's ingrained in me from years of living in The Grove, where just about everyone greets you when you see them. As I got closer, I noticed the man was about sixty years old, with a massive build augmented by steroids. His skin had that purple, bruised coloration that brings to mind tuna tartare, and I noticed his abdomen was bloated since his liver and kidneys had grown along with his pecs and bis. Upon closer inspection, I noticed he dyed his hair, eyebrows and beard black, and days in the sun had turned them a deep purple that just about matched his skin.

I said hello.

"Hi! How are you?" he replied, which I found interesting since some of the men in The Pines tend to scowl when you say hello.

"Oh, I'm fine!" I responded.

"What are you up to?" he asked.

"I'm going to meet some friends at Sip N Twirl," I said.

"Oh, nice! That sounds fun. You should come by and see my house first. We've got a great pool and a wet bar! You can make yourself a drink for the way over."

Slightly buzzed, and pretty sure I would wind up with a ridiculous story by the time this ended, I agreed.

"Sure! I can't stay long because I'm meeting friends at 8, but I have a few minutes," I told him.

"Great. It's just a few houses down," he said as we started towards his house.

Along the way, he introduced himself as Mark and before I knew it, we were there. The central part of his house was made of glass, and I could see the outdoor pool and deck directly through the living room.

"Right this way!" Mark said as we headed to his backyard. "So this is the pool," he said as he started his tour. "And right over here we have a wet bar. Would you like a drink?" he asked, as thoughts of getting roofied entered my head.

"I don't drink," I lied, hoping he didn't smell the vodka on my breath. "Oh, that's okay. My housemate is in AA, I get it," he said. "If you get thirsty, though, just let me know," Buffalo Bill — I mean – Mark said. I was starting to feel like one of the women in *Silence of the Lambs* must have felt seconds before they were thrown in the back of a van.

"And over here's the shed," he said as we made our way around the pool and to the side of the house. "It's really equipped with just about every tool you could imagine," he said as he smirked. "You should take a look!"

I opened one of the doors to the shed as a red light cast a shadow on my forearm. Oh, God. I really was in *Silence of the Lambs*.

As I pulled the door further open, I saw that the toolshed had been converted into a miniature sex dungeon. The entire thing was lit by a single red bulb hanging from the ceiling. To the right was an entire wall of dildos, which varied in size from semi-normal to *Oh-My-God-How-Can-Someone-Fit-That-Inside-Themselves?!?* On the left side of the shed/sex dungeon were whips and other sex toys. Directly in the center of the shed was a leather sling. Picture the playroom in *Fifty Shades of Grey* — but in a garden shed.

Mark sidled up next to me and opened the other side of the door so the entire shed — er — dungeon? was exposed. He sat down in the sling and leered at me.

"This can be a lot of fun, you know?" he whispered sensually as he leaned back and threw his legs in the air. Thankfully, he was wearing a square-cut bathing suit so I didn't have to see how much damage that construction cone-sized dildo probably did to his sure-to-be-gaping hole.

"Um I gotta go I'm late to meet my friends" I blurted as I made my way back towards the pool and through the house as fast as I could.

"Wait! Don't go! We could have a lot of fun!" he said. "You're cute! I would love to play with you in the dungeon!"

I could take no more. "Dungeon? That's a toolshed! And I'm not really into that!" I told him.

"Oh, calm down, Mary!" he snapped. "If it's not your thing, just say so! You don't have to get all hot and bothered about it!"

"Bye," I said as I bee-lined out of the house and onto the boardwalk.

A few minutes later, I was at Sip N Twirl, where I ran into friends and danced the night away. When the party ended, I wound up walking home with a neighbor who also lived in The Grove. As we got to the corner of Tuna Walk and Fire Island Boulevard, who did we run into but Mark, who was still working that corner like Donna Summer on the cover of "Bad Girls," trying to lure another victim to his garden shed.

"Hi! . . . Oh, it's *you*," he said as we made our way past him. For the first time in my life, I decided to break my rule of greeting everyone I passed, gave him a snarl and continued on my way.

CRYSTAL DUNGEONS

Years before I could afford a full season share in The Grove, I made the mistake of getting a quarter share with Bring It in The Pines. Since he was busiest on weekends because he owned a restaurant, the two of us looked for a midweek share when we would both be able get to the island. Since most people work nine to five, they're thrilled when guys come in who won't take up a bed on precious weekends. Especially since it helps offset the cost of a rental.

We started looking for places, and by the end of March, Bring It forwarded me a bunch of listings he found on Craigslist. After seeing pictures of a few ramshackle homes, he sent me a place that seemed too good to be true. It was oceanfront with a pool and a hot tub overlooking the beach. After contacting the guy running the house, we found out it would be empty during the week and signed right up. Before we wrote the checks, Bring It met with Tom, the "housemother," who said he was happy to have us on board. His last words to Bring It were that it was a "non-party house." An interesting choice of words before the term became ubiquitous in the gay community, but we didn't know what it meant yet and didn't care. We would never see these people.

On our first trip, Bring It pilfered his restaurant and brought out fish, vegetables, champagne, bottles of rosé and vodka. As soon as we got to the house, we headed straight for the kitchen to unpack our groceries and get the blender out for our first round of frozen margaritas. Two minutes later, a ripped, shirtless guy in his late 20s came strolling in. He was 6'4", dark-haired and stunning. He introduced himself as Rob and told us he was a friend of Tom's who would be crashing there for the week. Both our antennas went up, but he seemed like a nice guy, so we let it pass.

I asked him what he did for a living and he blushed.

"Uh . . . I'm an escort?" he said/asked.

"And to think I slave away in restaurants when I could be sucking dick," Bring It said.

We all laughed. Bring It always had a way of making people feel at ease. A few minutes later, Rob told us he was also a porn star. He had just finished shooting *The Men of Fire Island Part 3* that afternoon in the Meat Rack. We offered him a frozen margarita and invited him to lunch. He declined and popped open a Coke. Then he told us we could relax in the pool as he cleaned up the kitchen.

When we asked Rob to join us for dinner, he told us he was going to meet a friend. A few hours later, he came back with his friend and told us that he would be spending the night, too. When I asked how their dinner was, he said they just had drinks. We were abuzz about our new guest. Was he a client? How much would Rob charge for an overnight stay? Bring It thought Rob's friend was too young to be a client. If that was the case, what were they doing in that bedroom all night long? The answer came the next day.

Around noon, Bring It started looking for a ferry schedule so he could arrange a visit from our friend, Tim, aka whatchamacallit. I told him to check Rob's room, since he used one when his friend came the day before. Two minutes later, I heard Bring It calling for me.

"Greg, come in here!" he shouted.

Intrigued, I went in the bedroom and saw Bring It holding what looked like a crack pipe.

"Are they crack addicts?" I asked.

"Uh, no, dear. They're crystal queens."

Looking back, Rob showed all of the signs of a meth addict, which I would soon learn to spot: He was rail-thin, which came from *not eating*. He liked to talk *because he was wired out of his mind*. He drank Coke because *meth addicts crave sugar*. And he offered to clean the kitchen *because he was a speed freak*.

When we got back to the city, I called Tom.

"You told us no one would be at the house," I said.

"Oh, that was just a temporary situation. It won't be like that again," he said in a thick German accent. "I just had Rob stay there because we needed a maid. I figured I'd save some money and told him he could stay."

"But what about the fact that he was smoking meth and you told us it was a 'non-partying' house?" I asked him.

"Oh, I know Rob has a problem and I've tried to get him off of drugs time and again. But I promise you that this will not happen once more."

Sort of relieved, we decided to give the house another chance.

When we got to the house for our next visit, two men were lounging in the living room. They introduced themselves as Jay and Michael, and told us they were weekend shares who decided to stay the week.

"We *planned* on leaving Sunday, but after we smoked Tina, that went out the window," Jay said. "We haven't slept since Friday," he happily announced.

It was Tuesday.

"Junior Vasquez was spinning on Saturday at the Pavilion and he spun a flawless set. It took me on *such* a journey," he said.

I could tell.

"Then Sunday night, Tony Moran spun and, let me tell you, he was off. He was losing people left and right. No one was feeling his energy. By two o'clock, the place was dead," he added.

It was a Sunday night in June. Who was going to party until the sun came up when they needed to get back to work in the city the next day? The answer: crystal queens.

"So then Monday came and we decided to stay for the week. Fuck that job; if they let me go, I'll just collect unemployment for the next six months. I need to relax anyway."

I could tell.

Jay bounced around the kitchen — on the counter — on the table — then over to the living room, and back to the counter again. As I looked him in the eye, I saw a facial twitch that looked like the onset of Bells palsy. He downed a Coke and started gnawing on Swedish Fish. Michael just sat there in a catatonic state, drinking Coke and smiling like a half-witted baby. I was starting to realize some of the dungeons on Fire Island were made of crystal.

Bring It excused himself from the bizarre interactive one-man show we were watching to mix margaritas.

"Would you like one?" he asked Jay.

"Oh, no. Alcohol is poison. Who do you think is behind all those anti-crystal ads in Chelsea? Absolut. They're losing so much money now that everyone does crystal and they're trying to make it seem like it's a really bad drug, so people will go back to drinking. But I don't touch the stuff, it's horrible for your liver."

"Oh, really? Did you know they use paint thinner to make crystal?" Bring It asked. He roared with laughter. "More propaganda!"

"Anyway, Michael and I are now in recuperation mode, so we're heading to the bedroom to relax for the rest of the week. We'll see you later," Jay said.

Michael just smiled and followed him like a dog.

"Will you be joining us for dinner?" Bring It asked.

Jay roared with more laughter. "We don't *eat*. And besides, I could stand to lose a few. I feel fat."

I could see his ribs.

The speed freaks disappeared into their bedroom and Bring It turned to me and said, "I feel like I just got off the treadmill."

I put on some down-tempo music as we started making dinner. At six o'clock, a strange man came into the house while we were in the kitchen.

"Are you Jay?" he asked. "Uh, no, he's in the bedroom," Bring It replied.

The man went into their room. Fifteen minutes later, he was on his way again. Two minutes later, Jay burst out of his bedroom and ran over to the stereo.

"I need to lower this music. It's just *not* taking me on a journey," he snapped.

A journey? I was listening to Miguel Migs while cleaning lettuce.

"This Frankie Knuckles bullshit does nothing for me," he said, as he ran back to his room.

Half an hour later, we had another houseguest.

"Looking for Jay?" Bring It asked. "Uh huh," stuttered another crystal queen.

It soon became apparent Jay and Michael were setting up tricks every hour on the hour on Manhunt. This continued the rest of the night. As our *real* guests arrived, we told them about our elusive houseguests who were "recuperating" in their bedroom. Without fail, every hour on the hour, a new man came over to "fuck their holes" as they later told us.

As I was rinsing the plates after dinner, Jay came over and asked if he could borrow some condoms and lube. He and Michael had run out and were expecting a "guest" in a little while.

I asked how many he needed, and he said, "I don't know – ten, twelve? We just go through them so fast when we're in crystal bottom mode – you know?"

"No, but here you go," I said.

"Oh, you're the best. I'm so glad you and Bring It will be with us this season."

All night long, the front gate kept creaking open as more of their hookups came over. Too bad they didn't use any of that lube to grease the door's hinges. I finally fell asleep as the sun rose, only to be rudely awakened two hours later.

"This is my fucking vacation! Why are you trying to ruin it for me?!" Jay screamed at the top of his lungs.

My eyes snapped open as Michael tried to appease him.

"I don't know why you're carrying on. Just calm down and let's talk about this," he said.

"I will not calm down! And if you come one step closer, I'm calling the police and having you escorted off the island! I paid for this share and I'll make it my business you never step foot back on Fire Island Pines the rest of your life!" he raged.

"Please, let's just go for a walk and talk this over," Michael said.

They headed to the beach to settle their differences. As I watched from the deck, Jay carried on, throwing his hands in the air, inadvertently causing seagulls to flee.

By ten o'clock, they were back to their old selves: swilling Coke and talking incessantly.

"Sorry about that rage I had this morning. That always seems to happen when I'm on vacation. It must be pent-up anger from that job," Jay said.

So it has nothing to do with the fact that you haven't slept in four days, I thought.

"So what caused the fight?" I actually said.

"Well, Michael turned to me at eight o'clock and asked what I wanted to do today. I was livid! I mean I am on vacation! I don't want to plan out my day — whatever happens, happens. It's not like I'm going to access my PalmPilot on my Goddamn vacation."

"I just asked if you wanted to go to the beach," Michael said from the kitchen table, where he was eating gummy worms.

"Exactly," Jay said as he stormed into the bedroom.

Two minutes later, he frantically emerged from his room.

"I'm writing a manifesto to the housemother!" he announced. "There wasn't any toilet paper in the bathroom and that's not the way a house should be run. I've vacationed in Fire Island Pines since 1985 and this has never happened before! I refuse to live like this. Something must be done. Rules need to be set down."

Jay set up his laptop on the kitchen table and typed away the rest of the day. While we were carrying on in the pool, swimming in the ocean and having a great time, he spent his entire day writing his rant. At four o'clock, I looked up from my raft to see Bring It serving margaritas in drag. A few minutes later, Michael came out of his room with his bags.

"I'm leaving," he said as he stormed out the door.

"If I knew that would be his reaction, I would have thrown this wig on days ago," Bring It said.

As soon as Michael left, Jay ran over to us.

"Thank God he's gone. He brings me down. I mean he wouldn't stop complaining about how I forgot it was his birthday today. I mean how was I supposed to know what day it was? I haven't slept since Friday! For all I know, this could be Tuesday!"

It was Wednesday.

"Well, at least I can finally relax. I'll be inside finishing the manifesto," he said. His facial twitch had progressed and he now looked like he was getting electro-shock treatments.

A few hours later, the phone rang while we were having dinner.

"Can I speak to Jay? It's Michael."

"Hey, Michael, it's Greg – and by the way, Happy Birthday!" I said.

"Well at least *someone* remembered," he said.

"Well, hold on, I'll go get him."

As I got to Jay's door, another stranger emerged from his bedroom.

"Hey, Jay, Michael's on the -"

"I hate to get you involved in this, Greg, since we just met today . . ."

Actually, it was yesterday.

"But tell him I will not be talking to him on the phone until at least Friday. We just had a fight through email and I am *livid*."

It was nice to see his vacation was finally mellowing him out.

"Uh . . . okay?" I said.

When I told Michael the news, he was crushed. Truly saddened, I said, "I'm sorry you're going through this on your birthday. You seem like a nice guy." He hung up.

"I'm finally done with the manifesto!" Jay announced two hours later. "You and Bring It need to read it and sign it so I can send it to Tom!"

It was now eleven o'clock and I had been drinking since four. The last thing I wanted to do was read his ten-page manifesto. But he wasn't having any of it.

"I'll read it aloud!" he announced. He grabbed a handful of Swedish Fish and started reading his creed.

Twenty minutes later, he was finished.

Ten minutes before that, I had fallen asleep.

"So what do you guys think?" he asked.

"I think you need to take a Xanax and put that manifesto to bed, along with yourself," Bring It said. He was no longer wearing a wig, but his makeup made him look fierce.

"Maybe you're right. I'm gonna go online for a little while and catch some sleep," Jay said.

Two days later, he woke up. By that time, we were packing and trying to figure out how to get out of this hell-house. Just the idea of spending another week with these drug addicts was making *my* face start to twitch. As we were leaving, Jay hit me up for twenty dollars because Michael stole his wallet when he left. Twenty dollars was a small price to pay for my sanity, so I forked it over and we were on our way.

When I got back to Brooklyn, I was shocked when I got an email from Tom throwing *Bring It and me* out of the house! Apparently, after we left, Jay added a few more pages to his manifesto, complaining about "all the noise those alcoholics made with their unannounced overnight guests and loud drag parties." *This* from the person who raged all day and night, had "unannounced guests" in his bedroom every fifteen minutes, and wouldn't let *anyone* relax. Shocked, but also relieved to be out of that mess, Bring It and I decided to cut our losses and ask for half our money back. Tom agreed, and said he would mail us a check for $1,600. The check never arrived, so a month later, Paul, who just so happens to be a real estate attorney, served him with legal papers. A week later, he mailed us a check with this grammatically incorrect response:

> "Hi Bring It! The last I want is a lawsuit, and I really hope we can settle this in private. Here's my admission to this matter: When you and I sat down to sign that lease and you asked if the house was empty during weekdays, I said that sometimes you might be lucky and 'the house is yours'. Well, don't you think I didn't know what I said, Bring It, but in context to the summer share that I for the first time was managing here, has to deal with the simple and regular common rules. And once that escalated it was time for us to depart. That I then claimed to not return the half of your quarter share, is with due respect to my fellow housemates and especially those that felt violated here. Let's put it this way, I didn't have a pleasant summer in this house in regards to the shares, and especially yours but sure am not hear to keep money and than have you slap a lawsuit in my face. So, I do hope I can have this settled between you and me, and that I will send you a check of the agreed $1,600 back to you next week. I do not need a WAR here! In my business I have plenty of enemies and lawsuits. This should not be and I apologize, for your summer was also ending unpleasant. Please do take my apologies and please let's move on! Thanks!"

And to think we came across this listing on Craigslist . . .

Bring It in our tragic summer share. Yes, that's a VCR.

THE CRYSTAL METH CHALLENGE

I was inspired to make the following fictional entry my Facebook status after witnessing the behavior of an "artist"— aka crystal addict — who lives in Cherry Grove.

Day 378 of The CrysTal MeTh Challenge: Worked in The garden all nighT long Til 6am with a miner's lamp on my head killing mosqiTos with a Torch, Then resTarTed my 8Th day day day day wiTh a handful of gummy bears, a coke and a box of sugar. Today I am writing ThaT screenplay about geTTing fired from The Pavilion in 1998! After I finish The KicksTarTer page for my STarT up, wriTe ThaT song, email Trump and kill The Black Mold Demon ThaT lives in the bedroom closeT and biTes my face aT niTe! Stabbing pains in my lower back. STuTTering a loTTTTT. FUCK FUCK FUCK FUCK! No TeeTh but give great head now. Neeeeed mooooore sugar! HosTing a parTy This afTeenoon. NSA.

THE PINES PARTY

Say what you want about drug abuse, but addictions are not always cut-and-dry. I know a lot of people who became addicted to prescription pain meds whose lives fell apart; and others who get hooked on good, old-fashioned "street drugs" who lead normal lives. If you want proof, look no further than Fire Island, which is *riddled* with semi-functioning meth heads. Although you'd think they'd be a mess, many of them hold steady jobs, have great work ethics, and always smile when you see them on the boards.

As years go by, they all wind up with that same gaunt look that comes from their teeth falling out, and inevitably turn into people who talk more than my bipolar cousin after she downs a Red Bull. I know it might seem strange if you haven't experienced it, but a lot of these people are sweet and normal. In my years on the island, I've met a lot of crystal addicts, and it just seems wrong to judge people who find themselves in a situation they can't get out of when they're decent and hardworking.

One of my favorite meth heads on the island is a gardener named Jonathon who's as funny as he is toothless. Although he's used drugs for years, I recently found out he's a veteran who suffers from PTSD, so who am I to judge? Maybe he uses meth to help relieve whatever pain he's going through.

For some reason, the two of us always wind up working together when we volunteer to help set up The Pines Party, a huge fundraiser that takes place on the beach every July. Hotels, homeowners, restaurants and bars all profit from it, and I like to volunteer to help set it up because ~~I want a free ticket~~ my friends produce it.

On the day we volunteer, Jonathon and I always wind up doing some kind of manual labor because all the other queens just want to sit around decorating tents and shit. Without fail, he always offers me a bump of crystal when I see him at 10 AM, which I decline.

"Suit yourself, buddy! But it's gonna be a lot easier hauling this shit across the sand with a boost!" he'll say with his signature toothless smile.

One year, the two of us were tasked with hauling a bunch of stakes to the beach so we could build snow fencing around the party. While we were loading up a truck, Jonathon accidentally left his cell phone on a bench. Later that day, when I brought the truck back to the harbor for another load, I spotted a phone case labeled "Jonathon's cell phone" on the bench. I laughed, pocketed the phone and headed back to give it to him.

"Hey. Why did you write 'Jonathon's phone case' on this?" I asked when I handed it to him.

"Honey, I label everything! When your brain is as scrambled as mine is, you'd be amazed where you wind up leaving things!" he said. "You should see what I do with my drugs! I bought one of those pill cases. And in each compartment, I put coke, ketamine and Tina. I never mark which one is which cuz when I think I'm gonna have a bump of crystal and it winds up being K, I just know it's gonna be a good day!"

I laughed and we started pounding the stakes in the sand.

Later that week, I ran into Jonathon while he was leaving a porta potty during the party.

"Baby, I think *everyone* got their powders mixed up tonight because those bathrooms smell like the ninth circle of hell! You want a bump of Tina?"

"No, but thanks," I said.

"Suit yourself!" he said as he kissed me on the cheek and

headed to the dance floor.

As he was walking away, my drag daughter, Tara Hole Jenkins (aka Chad) stumbled up to me on a mix of acid, mushrooms, molly, coke and . . . Viagra? (The next day, I found out he took Viagra because "Hey, you never know!") He told me to wait for him by the porta potties so we could grab a drink when he was done. *Fifteen minutes later*, when he had yet to come out, I walked over, knocked on the door and shouted, "Are you in there?"

He frantically responded a second later. "Oh my God!! I've been trying to get out of here for an hour, but I can't find the door!"

I started knocking and told him to follow the sound of my banging so he could figure out where the damn door was. When he finally emerged, he sweating like a maniac.

He wiped his forehead. "Oh my God, that was awful! I kept seeing lights flashing through the top of this thing, but they didn't last long enough for me to find the door! That was a nightmare!"

Needless to say, experiences like these make me realize that my decision to stop doing drugs twenty years ago was definitely for the best.

Chad and me in our "Wizard of Oz" flying monkey costumes before he got lost in a porta potty on a combination of acid, mushrooms, molly, coke and Viagra.

MOLLY, WE HAVE A PROBLEM

Although I've *severely* lowered my drug intake over the years, I'd be a liar if I didn't admit I occasionally still do drugs. This usually happens out of desperation, like, say, when I'm wasted at three in the morning and someone tells me they have a bag of coke. I can always tell when I start slurring when I'm drinking, and by that point — it's either do a bump of coke or stumble home.

Every once in a while, I'll also make the mistake of listening to my pot-head friends who convince me to take a hit of weed, even though I gave it up years ago because it makes me tired and paranoid. Don't get me wrong. Smoking weed always brings on fun times — like the night we decided to rearrange our living room at 2 AM. Or the time we became obsessed with Elektra Abundance's character on FX's Pose and started spewing her lines at one other with bad living room drag on.

"I'm a full woman now!" I said to my friends wearing a kimono in Elektra's stilted fashion.

"Bye, bye, brick!" Carl shouted back with a towel wrapped around his head.

While I always wind up doing a little coke or weed here and there, I haven't done ecstasy since I gave it up in the '90s. Sadly, I never got to try her sister, Molly, because she started hitting the clubs a few years later. Besides, I had a lot of bad experiences with ecstasy — like all those times at Body & Soul — and I had no interest in trying this new, "improved" version.

Of course, after years of cajoling from just about everyone I knew, I did wind up trying Molly at The Pines Party in the summer of 2018. I was really nervous about doing it, so I made sure my friends and I got there before it kicked in. I wanted to be able to get through the door, say hello to everyone I knew, and do it on the dance floor ensconced in a sea of shirtless men in case I turned into a mess. My friends put up with me being totally neurotic about this, and we finally took it around midnight.

Forty-five minutes after popping the capsule, it hit me. My body broke out in a huge sweat, and my head started feeling heavy and weird. A few minutes later, I got so fucking high I needed to get off the dance floor so I could sit on the sand like some kind of weirdo. I'm telling you, drugs affect my weird, gimp system different from anybody else I know. I can't take Sudafed without becoming suicidal, and apparently Molly makes me so damn high, I can hardly talk. And there was no way I wanted to run into anyone I knew without being able to make sentences, so I sat on the sand for an hour *like a total fucking loser*. A doctor once told me my body metabolizes medicine differently from most people, which at least explains why this happens to me all the time.

Six hours later, I was still high as a kite. Adding insult to injury, the sun started to rise, and my eyes were dilated like a crackhead's. At this point, my friends and I decided to call it a night and walk home on the beach. The ocean and sand had turned amber, and sandpipers were flitting all about. Sunrise is always magical on Fire Island, and the Molly made that walk home even more so. Those early morning walks after The Pines Party are some of my favorite memories on Fire Island. The beach turns peaceful, and the only time I get to see it at that hour is when I'm coming home from that party either drunk, or, in this case, high. Cuz you know my ass does not get out of bed before 8 AM *ever*.

When my friends and I finally got home, we put on Sade's *Diamond Life* and shared a bottle of wine. I closed my eyes and realized I was finally feeling all lovey-dovey and chill, like I hoped I'd be feeling all night. One of my friends suggested we take a Xanax to unwind, and let's just say I have never felt more unwound in my entire life. An hour later, I passed out and woke up at three in the afternoon.

Then I started popping a bunch of SAM-e cuz you know my gimp-ass self would totally get that post-Molly depression everyone talks about and I did not need to feel all suicidal like that time I took Zyrtec.

CHECK, PLEASE

A friend of mine who lives on Fire Island decided to deal with his lifelong drinking problem by joining AA a few years ago. Part of me was upset because we would (probably?) never share another evening like the time he unzipped his pants, took his penis out and placed it in the glass of a woman who was complaining about not having enough olives in her martini.

With his dick in her drink, he looked down and said, "Many people find this garnish a lot tastier," and cracked up laughing, along with the rest of the bar.

For someone who had hit rock bottom time and again, I wondered what finally made him sober up.

When I asked, he relayed the following story: One night, after drinking at a bar in The Pines, he went back to his apartment in The Grove through the Meat Rack. As he made his way through the woods, he came across a strapping black man. He sidled up next to him and asked, "So how's it going tonight, big guy?" When the man ignored him, he snapped, "So it's going to be like that, huh?" and stormed off. As he brushed past this hunk, he realized he was talking to a plastic bag that had blown into a tree. He hasn't had a drink since.

EQUAL OPPORTUNITY

While Fire Island has the Meat Rack for men to cruise in for anonymous sex and herpes, Massachusetts' gay vacation destination Provincetown has the Dick Dock. Located underneath a pier at the edge of town, the Dick Dock is teeming with sex just about every night of the summer. Although I spend most of my season on Fire Island, I like to escape to P-Town every August for a change of pace. Up until a few years ago, I had a gay cousin who lived there, and I'd spend my time helping him in his jewelry studio and having dinner with him at the end of the day.

My cousin Frankie was larger than life in both spirit and size. When I was a child, I was magnetically drawn to him. Although I didn't know what gay meant yet, I knew we had something in common from very early on. Frankie knew I was gayer than glitter the second I popped out of my mother's vagina, and started showering me with Grace Jones and Village People records when I was just a kid. He once told me *every single one of his relatives* knew he was gay since he was two years old, something that annoyed him since he was never able to have a "Coming Out" party.

He'd always rant about this whenever I saw him. "I mean, what the hell was I gonna come out from? I used to style my sister's hair and play with her dolls when I was in kindergarten! It doesn't get any gayer than that! Then, after high school, I wanted a big Coming Out party like some of my friends, but everyone already knew I was gay! All my friends got to have parties. But not me. It's really wasn't fair, Greg. At. All."

I would just stare at him, wondering why this grown man was obsessed with having a Coming Out party, something I had never even *heard* of.

He'd go on: "Now that I think about it, my whole life has been a party, and half those fags are dead."

As someone who lost a lot friends in the '80s, Frankie's way of dealing with tragedies like the AIDS crisis was through humor. It's one of the things that helped him get through life as a big, flaming homo without every being harmed. It's hard for people to attack you if you're making them laugh — something I, too, learned early on.

Frankie was one of the zaniest people I've ever met. For a while, he drove around the country in an RV and would stay wherever he wanted. Before he landed in Provincetown, he lived in Santa Fe, San Francisco and New Orleans. He lived a carefree life and never once thought about playing by society's rules.

When Frankie finally landed in P-town, he used to drive his vintage Cadillac at fifty miles an hour, even though some of the streets in P-town are only two feet wider than his car. He'd have his head turned to me the entire time telling me stories, and I'd pray we'd make it out of that thing alive. Then, in the '90s, he bought a boat and he'd drive it around the harbor in drag, pull up to tea dances, drop his anchor, and pour himself a martini. When he wasn't in drag, he was wearing a long dreadlock wig capped off with a giant hat because it made him seem "exotic" to his clients. He was ridiculous.

When Frankie began pursuing jewelry making full-time, he changed his name to Franco because, "People assume I'm an artist from Italy, and not some poor fag from Long Island. They eat that kind of shit up! And now, I charge whatever I want. You see this bracelet? This thing cost four bucks to make and now I charge one hundred and twenty-five for it."

Whenever I'd visit, he'd make us martinis when he cooked dinner. When we were done eating, he'd pass out watching TV as I cleaned up. Most nights, I'd go to the bars by myself for a few hours, even though Boston gays can be cliquey. I'd usually wind up drinking alone and heading home a few hours later after talking to, like, no one.

One night, after stopping for a slice of pizza on the way home, I decided to drop by the Dick Dock. My heart was pumping through my unbuttoned shirt as I came across a huddled mass of men having sex in a giant swarm underneath the dock. Oddly, the first thing that came to mind was not a mind-blowing porn, but *Night of the Living Dead*. Everyone lurched back and forth, in a variety of positions, without uttering a word. It was bizarre.

That's the thing about the Dick Dock: no one speaks. The only sounds you hear are the occasional "uh uh" and a slurp or two. Which only adds to the whole "zombies feeding" aura. Call me crazy, but I think a "So, what's up?" serves as a perfect introduction before you put my dick in your mouth.

I made sure there was a full moon the night I went so I could see the faces of anyone I might engage in a sex act with so I didn't wind up going down on Mike Pence. Needless to say, the only action I got was when some old man grabbed my crotch as he eased his way out of the snake pit.

This wound up being a blessing, because five minutes later, the police showed up and blasted the area with floodlights. You can imagine my disgust when I realized some of these men were actually in *Night of the Living Dead*. The original one.

That trip to the Dick Dock stayed with me a long time. I began to wonder, why aren't there places lesbians go to hook up? Did women feel the urge to have sex with strangers in outdoor places like men did? Could this place exist? In short, where was the Pussy Pier?

The Pussy Pier! A magical land where lesbians sit around a campfire sharing intimate details about their formative years until they become emotionally bonded enough to go down on one another! Dream catchers would fly in the wind along with cans of Bud Light and jeans from Sam's Club! Poetry readings would end with cunnilingus sessions! Bolo ties would be cast aside as dental dams were procured! Weddings would take place during post-coital spooning sessions on the sand!

For some reason, I just don't see this happening.

SOUTHERN DECADENCE

One of Fire Island's long-reigning drag queens, Porsche, spends her summers performing at the Ice Palace and her winters in Key West. Porsche is known for spot-on impressions of Amy Winehouse, Ariana Grande, Janis Joplin and countless others. I've known her a long time, and hold a special place in my heart for drag queens who have a talent besides lip-stinking to Beyoncé. Whether you're a comedian like Bianca Del Rio, a song parodist like Sherry Vine, or a singer like Porsche, I highly respect drag queens who work on their craft as much as their contour.

Porsche has a kind smile that instantly puts people at ease. Unlike other drag queens who can be competitive, Porsche invites other singers and queens to guest in her shows and loves watching them perform as she sips a Jack and Coke at the bar. I see her perform a few times every summer, and we always hang out after her show ends.

For years, Porsche would bring up Key West whenever I hung out with her.

"I can't believe you and Paul have never been there, Greg! You will just love it! It's right up your alley. It's one *hell* of a town!"

I wasn't familiar with Key West, aside from the fact that it was a party town with lots of gay bars and drag shows. After years of hearing about Key West from Porsche and other Fire Island friends, Paul and I decided to check it out. Porsche also told me how beautiful the drive through the Keys was, so we flew into Miami and rented a convertible for the five-hour drive down. Of course, Key West — like so many gay vacation destinations like Fire Island and Provincetown — is completely out of the way.

That's one thing I hate about gay vacation spots. Since most of them were founded as outposts where gays could be open and free without fear of attack, they were created in remote places. The Cape? Let's make them go to Provincetown — the last fucking town at the end of that curlicue. New York? Let's make them take a twenty-minute ferry ride to Fire Island after riding the Long Island Railroad for an hour. The Keys? Let's choose *the last fucking one.*

I really shouldn't complain. The drive through the Keys was stunning. Miles of azure-blue water and sky for as far as the eye could see interspersed with cute little towns with names like Key Largo and the appealing-sounding Key Ramrod. *Yes, please.*

When we finally arrived in Key West, the first thing I noticed was that there were homeless people everywhere — the tannest homeless people I'd ever seen. Everywhere I looked, I saw tan homeless people sitting on the streets, begging for change, stumbling around in drunken hazes and trying to hustle people. It made sense: If I were homeless, I'd be in Key West, too — enjoying the weather and living off the fat of happily buzzed tourists. Not living in NYC trying to get quarters out of angry, cold commuters on the F train.

Unfortunately, the weather sucked the week we visited. A storm had recently rolled through and it was freezing when we got to the clothing-optional resort we booked. I was initially hesitant to stay at one because I've never been one for clothing-optional *anything*. In my experiences, men who are attracted to clothing-optional resorts should actually vacation in clothing *mandatory* resorts. For every chiseled Adonis, there are 300 warped and grizzled Gollums — the kind of men you'd see asking for a riddle to cross a bridge or stumbling around the streets on *The Walking Dead.*

But since we had never stayed in a clothing-optional resort before, we decided to give it a shot. Sadly, the pool deck was filled with the aforementioned Gollums, so Paul and I decided to book a snorkeling trip we saw advertised in the local gay rag. I love going on gay tours because that's when you get a chance to meet the most interesting LGBTQs from around the world you might not meet otherwise.

Sadly, the day of our snorkeling trip, we were the only two on the boat besides the captain. Unbeknownst to us, the storm had turned the water murky, and brought in subarctic water the two of us would soon discover was similar to the temperatures the people on The Titanic suffered through. But since we hadn't figured that out yet, we jumped right in when the captain dropped anchor. As soon as we hit the water, the life drained from our faces. I tried to be a good sport and splashed around the brown-tinged water for a few minutes so the captain didn't think I was a pussy, but when I looked over and saw Paul's face turning purple, I decided enough was enough.

"Let's get out! I'm freezing!" I screamed.

"You think?" Paul chattered back.

When the captain pulled us onto the boat, I looked over and saw Paul's entire chest had turned purple, too. Both our bodies were shivering and, in a sick twist of fate, clouds had rushed in and the sun was nowhere to be found.

"So how was it?" Captain Fuckface asked.

Not one to lie, I said, "That was the worst snorkeling trip I've ever been on in my life. I'm so cold right now, my penis is in my stomach and I didn't see one damn fish!"

He laughed and said he knew it wasn't the best day for snorkeling, but didn't want to ruin our plans. *Really, girl?*

When we got back to the hotel, the two of us were still in the midst of hypothermia. Paul suggested we warm up in the hot tub. We peeled off our still-freezing bathing suits and headed to the Jacuzzi. When we got there, we were thrilled to find we were the only ones around. We slid into the water and breathed a sigh of relief as our body temperatures started climbing out of the teens.

Just when we were falling into a state of pure relaxation, we heard a voice.

"Hoo-whee boy this is gonna feel fine as wine!"

The two of us looked up and saw one of those thin homeless men standing over us. Naked. He smiled, revealing a mouthful of charcoal-encrusted teeth that had obviously been discolored from years of smoking Marlboro Reds. Needless to say, he was sex incarnate.

"My name's Charlie!" he announced as he slid into the hot tub between us and stretched his arms out. "I come from Tennessee and I've been dreaming of getting my haunches in this hot tub all week long! I drive a rig full-time and let's just say my ass feels like it's been ridden by ten hot studs right about now!" he scream-shouted with a thick Southern accent that brought *Hee-Haw* to mind. He stretched out further so both his hands were touching our shoulders. "I don't know about you boys, but I could just about suck two cocks right about now!"

This was not happening. Although the blue collar fantasy of having a truck driver go down on me in a hot tub *was* appealing, the thought of that person being *Charlie* just turned it into a sick, twisted nightmare that would scar me for the rest of my life.

Not wasting any time, I told him, "We're in a closed relationship. We don't play with other guys."

"Well wouldn't that just be my luck!" he said. "Two fine young Eye-talian men from New York City, and the two of them wildly in love! I've been told I can suck the chrome off a trailer hitch and you don't know what in Hades you're missing, but suit yourselves!"

"I'm gonna get out. I'm starting to overheat," I told Paul, who took the hint and decided to get out, too.

"Well, it was nice meeting you, Charlie," Paul said. "I hope you find those two cocks you're looking for," he added as Charlie reached over and tugged on our dicks.

"Looks like I already did!" he said as he started guffawing. The two of us double-timed it out of that hot tub like we were in an old-timey cartoon and headed back to our room.

"What are our chances?" I asked Paul when we got back to the room. "People come to Key West and have orgies with hot guys — but we get hit on by Charlie! "

"That's fine," Paul said. "You're the only one I want to have sex with anyway," he said as he leaned over and kissed me. (Feel free to vomit.)

The next summer, I ran into Porsche while I was getting off the ferry one day.

"Soooo . . . how was Key West?!" she asked.

As I recalled images of malformed naked men, skinny homeless people and Charlie, I said, " . . . I guess you could say it was just like Cherry Grove."

"You see!" she said. "I *knew* you'd love it!"

Carl, Porsche and a cross-eyed Levonia after one of Porsche's show.

DRAG FOR DAYS

In 2018, you can catch a drag show every night of the week on Fire Island. Sometimes, three or four. It's as if the entire town has forgotten how to dance and only know how to scream, "Yaaas Queen WERK!" as a drag queen lip-synchs to a mash-up of Beyoncé, Sia and a speech from Mo'Nique's character in *Precious*. Some of the highlights include the Pool Show at the Ice Palace, where Logan Hardcore, Brenda Dharling and Ariel Sinclair entertain audiences as they perform around a pool; Cherry Bombed at Cherry's, where Busted challenges people with her deranged, yet intelligent drag; Porsche's live singing act at the Ice Palace, and Hedda Lettuce, who puts a smile on people's faces with witty commentary about life on Fire Island.

Toss in more shows from Honey Davenport, Pixie Aventura, Bubbles D'Boob, Holly Box-Springs, Tina Burner, Boudoir LeFleur and Kimmi Moore and you've got a lot of wig hair being tossed in the wind for birds to make their nests out of. Cuz that's a thing.

And although you'd think I would be the biggest champion of drag shows, it's starting to feel like too much of a thing. Part of me misses the days when you could show up at a bar to dance, talk to your friends or meet people without feeling you're being rude to a performer who's whipping her synthetic hair back and forth. Thankfully, the island still has Sip N Twirl, where you can dance and drink just about every night of the week, where the only drag queen you'll run into is Bubbles D'Boob, who hosts a few parties where you can laugh, dance *and* enjoy drag at the same time.

BINGO: WHERE DRAG QUEENS GO TO DIE

Call me hateful, but nothing depresses me more than when a drag queen friend tells me she got a gig hosting bingo. *Or* when one of my friends tells me that playing bingo is fun. Cuz if you're hosting bingo, it means you've reached rock bottom, and if you enjoy *playing* bingo, it means you're a raging alcoholic who will use any excuse to hang out in a bar. Sound harsh? Sorry not sorry, sort of sorry if you host bingo and read this? Love, Judge Judy.

MISS FIRE ISLAND

The unofficial end of the season in Cherry Grove is the Miss Fire Island pageant, which takes place the weekend after Labor Day at the Ice Palace. A huge affair, the event draws hundreds of people from all over Long Island — the majority of them straight. For some bizarre reason, this pageant attracts a very particular kind of audience known in some circles as "white trash." While there are drag shows and pageants all summer long, this is the only one that seems to attract these people in droves. They arrive by ferry, by boat, and by land — walking as far as four miles away from Ocean Beach to ogle the gay clowns in drag.

Miss Fire Island is a major production and runs over four hours long. It's also the town's last big hoorah before people start saying goodbye for the winter. By the time it arrives, I've already started looking forward to moving back home. As someone who doesn't do well in the humidity, the last two weeks of August are insufferable. It always seems to be three weeks of 90-degree weather with 93-percent humidity. Cue the salt pills. That, along with three months of drinking, DJing, and doing drag starts taking it's toll and I start longing for my air conditioned apartment back in Brooklyn around the third week of August. By the time Labor Day hits, I am *done*.

A lot of people on the island know about "Ugly August" — that time of year when fights break out between housemates and coworkers who have been toiling away all summer long under intense conditions. It's when people get fired, house mothers throw shares out, and people finally tell off that terrible drunk who's been ruining everyone's fun all summer long.

Another island tradition is "Sleep With Your Sister September" when, for some reason, coworkers and friends decide to hook up? But I honestly think this is a thing simply because of the alliteration and not too many people actually do it.

Thankfully, I usually return to work at *Saturday Night Live* the Tuesday after Labor Day, and memories of Ugly August and Sleep with Your Sister September fade away by the time all the waiters start blowing one another. The weekend after Labor Day, I head back for one last trip before my work schedule keeps me from coming back until the next spring.

It's also the weekend everyone in Cherry Grove puts aside their differences to rile against the hordes of Jerry Springer audience members who descend on the town for the Miss Fire Island contest. If you dare to venture downtown on the day of the contest, you'll find yourself surrounded by hordes of obnoxious, drunk people chain-smoking menthol cigarettes and drinking from plastic cups. Then again, that's basically every trip to Cherry Grove, but on *this* day, it's *straight* people doing it! Nothing against straight people, but this particular crowd is gross. I can't envision a trailer park across the bay, but obviously one exists.

Despite the crowd, Miss Fire Island is well regarded in the drag community, and many queens I know have taken home prizes over the years. Charity Charles, China, Porsche, Gusty Winds, Zola, Logan Hardcore and countless other queens have all snatched crowns at some point in their careers. And year after year, they all show up while drunk soccer moms with light-up tiaras and their beer-swilling, cigar-smoking, common-law husbands cheer them on.

I always stay home, because going into town that day is like going to a Trump rally. I'd much rather sip a few cocktails on the deck and watch as drunk "straight" men march down Lewis Walk in hopes of getting blown in the Meat Rack. Thankfully, by 8 PM, the competition ends and most of the crowd goes home. But there are always a few hangers-on who make going into town unbearable all night long.

The next day, the Ice Palace holds a coronation ceremony, where everyone from town is invited to watch the winning queens walk and/or perform. It's always a fun day, as most of the deplorables have receded back to their homes in Happauge. It's mainly just locals, and it's always fun to trade bitchy comments with friends about the girls' $900 human hair wigs and expensive gowns.

Later that day, everyone heads off the island for the week. Or, in my case, the year. The weekend after Labor Day marks the official end to my Fire Island season, and after the coronation, I pack up my wigs and speedos before taking that final ferry ride back to Brooklyn. Most homeowners and renters continue coming out until the end of October, and I'm always jealous when I see the sunset pictures they post on social media. September and October bring the nicest weather. Temperatures are usually in the high seventies, the sun is strong, and the ocean can be invitingly warm. As the season change and the Earth spins on it's access, the sun makes it's transit from setting over the bay to going down over the ocean and it's spectacular.

The Pines has their biggest post-season party at Sip N Twirl over Halloween weekend, and come November, most homeowners close up their houses after Thanksgiving weekend. But in recent years, more and more people have been keeping their homes open to enjoy chilly weekends with a fireplace burning day and night. If you ever get a chance, visit during the off-season. Pack some red wine, a flask, and of course, a faux-fur coat and synthetic wig. After all, you don't want to catch a cold — or a cold sore — in the Meat Rack.

BACK TO REALITY

One of the most beautiful things about living Cherry Grove is that people always say hello when you see them. I always feel like I'm on *The Waltons* when strangers greet me when I pass them on the boardwalk. Then Labor Day passes and I move back to Brooklyn, where the only person who says hello to me is that homeless woman looking for money outside the York Street subway station.

But for two weeks, I'll keep saying hello to people who look at me like I'm some kind of maniac. They'll scowl, or give me the side-eye, or a look I can only interpret as, "Are you a Jehovah's Witness?" Sometimes, they'll actually respond with things like, "Do I know you?" or my personal fave, "Shut up, fag." That's usually when I start counting the months until I move back to Fire Island.

Don't get me wrong. It's never easy to leave the island that last time, knowing I will not be back until Memorial Day weekend the next year. During our last week of the summer, Paul and I always have dinner parties with friends and wind up talking about all the fun we had that summer. There's always a bit of sadness when the season ends, and I try to be strong when I tell friends, "What can I do? I have to work all season so I can afford to live here next summer."

While I know that's true, I'm just putting up a front so our last weekend can be filled with good times. But the truth of the matter is that I always tear up as I ride across the Great South Bay for the last time, while swiping through all the pictures I've snapped on my iPhone that summer, knowing it will be nine months until I'm able to return back to the island of misfit boys . . .

ABOUT THE AUTHOR

Greg Scarnici is a comedic writer, director, producer, actor, DJ and musician whose videos have been viewed over 10 million times on YouTube and a host of other sites. His work has also been featured on MTV, VH1, Fox News and CNN. He currently works as an Associate Producer at *Saturday Night Live* as well as in various other capacities in theater, film and nightlife. Books include his debut collection of humorous essays: *I Hope My Mother Doesn't Read This* and *SEX IN DRAG*, a parody of Madonna's infamous *SEX* book.

Film credits include writing and directing the award-winning indie, *Glam-Trash*, the short films, *Dead End* and *Children of the Dune* as well as other shorts that have played at festivals around the country. He has also directed music videos for Kris Menace, The Kiki Twins, Jipsta, Mike Diamond, Pandora Boxx, Sherry Vine and others.

Acting credits include appearances in *30 Rock, Online Nation, Nick Cannon: Short Circuitz* and *A Star is Born*. Greg has also written and performed the shows, *Queens, The Buddy & Barbara Comedy Hour, Sex Tape, Must Be The Music* and *Gender Fluids* at Joe's Pub, Ars Nova, The UCB Theater, The Cavern Club Celebrity Theater in LA, The Oasis in San Franciso, The AllWays Lounge in New Orleans and at the Ice Palace and The Community House on Fire Island.

Check out www.gregscarnici.com to see some of his work and to hear some of the music he has released as himself, his drag alter ego, Levonia Jenkins, and his band, Undercover.

CPSIA information can be obtained
at www.ICGtesting.com
Printed in the USA
LVHW092256150319
610881LV00001B/70/P

9 781793 186669